The Sovereign Manifesto

JOHNNY MANNAZ

Divine Rite
The Sovereign Manifesto

Johnny Mannaz
Copyright © 2023

Book design by www.delaney-designs.com

All rights reserved. No part of this book may be used or reproduced by any means, graphic, electronic, or mechanical, including photocopying, recording, taping or by any information storage retrieval system without the written permission of the author except in the case of brief quotations in critical articles and reviews.

ISBN Softcover: 978-1-7345713-6-3

1.) Spirituality-Solar, 2.) Self-Actualization (Psychology),
3.) Sociology, 4.) Jurisprudence

LIVE YOUR WILL@www.thekingscurriculum.com

Table of Contents

Foreword 9

DIVINE RITE: The Sovereign Manifesto 11

1. True Will: A Law for All 17
2. Spiritual Sovereignty: One under the Sun 35
3. The Sovereign Process: Self-Actualization 51
4. Sovereign Politick: A legitimate critique 63
5. The Sovereign Nation: A New Dawn 95
6. Writing your own Declaration of Independence and Constitution 99
7. The Sovereign Sun 111
8. Sovereign Ethics 119
9. Sovereign Consciousness 127
10. The New Nobility 139
11. Declaration of the Sovereign Nation 143

Epilogue 153

Oath of the Spiritual Sovereign 155

This book is dedicated to the question:

"What is legitimate authority?"

Foreword

In an age where the world seems more complex and uncertain than ever before, it is human nature to yearn for guidance and stability. We search for answers to questions like, what will be our future place in the world? What values should we hold dear? How do we govern ourselves justly? Who or what represents legitimate authority?

In "*Divine Rite: The Sovereign Manifesto*," we will take up these questions and offer a compelling vision for how we might answer them. Drawing on history, philosophy, and a deep understanding of humanity's innate political and spiritual nature, this book brings our attention to the necessity of sovereignty for both individuals and nations.

While these ideas may seem archaic or outdated to some, this Manifesto presents a persuasive case that they are not only relevant, but crucial for a healthy society. This Manifesto asserts that the pursuit of sovereignty can lead to greater prosperity, stability, and meaning for civilization as a whole.

At a time when we face many challenges as a society, "*Divine Rite: The Sovereign Manifesto*" offers a bold and provocative vision, built upon self-evident truths, for how we might navigate these complexities. It is a perspective that demands our attention and invites us to think deeply about the nature of authority and its role in our lives.

This work is presented with the conviction that the ideas contained have much to offer readers who are both seeking answers to some of the most pressing questions of our time, *and* who are themselves willing to play an important role in the regeneration of civilization.

DIVINE RITE

THE SOVEREIGN MANIFESTO

At its heart, this manifesto is about affirming the most noble form of life you can live.

This manifesto is not about a political or religious agenda, but rather the Individual's own personal power and autonomy. It is a call to awaken to the truth of our being, to question the status quo and to reject the notion that we are mere subjects to be controlled, manipulated and ruled by nefarious institutions. It is a call to embrace our own sovereignty, to realize that we can become the masters of our own destiny and to live accordingly.

The Sovereign Manifesto promotes the idea that individuals possess a Divine Right to rule over their own consciousness as guided by their True Will. This means that individuals have the ultimate authority and responsibility for their own lives and actions, and should strive to discover and fulfill their own unique purpose and destiny.

The Sovereign Manifesto is a powerful call to action, a revolutionary new perspective on personal power and autonomy, encouraging individuals to discover their unique purpose and fulfill it by taking control of their own lives.

In this book, you will explore the importance of self-discovery, the dangers of external control, the responsibilities of self-rule, and the path to self-actualization. You will be challenged to question the nature of your reality and to reject the false narratives of authority that have been imposed upon you.

Through a combination of spiritual anecdotes, historical examples, and practical exercises, *The Sovereign Manifesto* will inspire you to break free from external influences and reclaim your autonomy as a self-ruler.

The Sovereign Manifesto is about the importance of having an independent soul, a free conscience, and the willingness to do what you must to keep this freedom.

This includes escaping the spider's web of ideas, institutions or political conceptions that seek to diminish human dignity through covert acts of "consensual" slavery.

The outline of this book is a general, overhead map of the battlefield with essential landmarks to serve as orientation. Upon this battlefield will occur a mythic clash to settle age old discrepancies between freedom and authority, power and restraint.

This manifesto is also a field manual designed to help the Individual gain a basic conceptual comprehension of Sovereignty: what it is, why it's valuable and what it takes to attain and maintain it.

Consider this book as a battle cry, a call to realize the power of your **True Will** and align your actions with it, to develop a critical and independent mindset, to build resilience against manipulation and take responsibility for your own life.

This manifesto suggests a holistic approach to self-actualization, by also addressing the importance of physical, mental, emotional and spiritual well-being, as well as the role of the individual in society.

The Sovereign Manifesto is an essential guide for anyone seeking to live a more authentic and fulfilling life. It is a call for humanity to reject the notion that we are nothing more than unwitting subjects in a vast, technocratic experiment.

It is a call to embrace our own Sovereignty, to realize that we have a God-given right, a Divine Right, to become masters of our own destiny, and to live our lives accordingly.

This is a book that will change the way you see the world, and help you to create a life rich with meaning. It's a must-read for anyone who wants to live a life of purpose, autonomy, and higher fulfillment.

Manifesting Sovereignty

The Sovereign Manifesto is the official call to arms for individuals everywhere to reclaim their inherent Divine Right.

The concept of **Divine Right** refers to the belief that individuals possess a natural and inalienable authority to govern their own lives, free from external manipulation, coercion and control. The Sovereign Individual is one who recognizes and responsibly exercises this right, taking full command of their own thoughts, actions, and decisions.

Throughout this manifesto, we will seek to answer that ancient question with an equally ancient answer, "what represents *legitimate* authority?"

Self-discovery is the key to understanding our True Will and the role it plays in achieving self-sovereignty. It is a journey that requires courage, honesty, and commitment, but it is a journey that is well worth taking. By discovering our True Will, we can begin to live our lives with purpose and direction, taking our rightful place as self-rulers of our own inner cosmos.

Being strong enough to resist the coercion of external forms of control is essential to becoming a Sovereign Individual. Through a saturation of media, society has become a matrix of pernicious external forces that seek to shape our beliefs, values, and perception in ways that fundamentally limit our freedom and autonomy. It is only by developing a critical and independent mindset, building resilience against manipulation and taking responsibility for our own lives that we can break free from external influences and reclaim our autonomy as self-rulers.

Self-rule is the ultimate expression of the Divine Right of the Individual, but it comes with certain responsibilities and obligations. By taking ownership of our actions and decisions, striving for self-actualization, respecting the autonomy of others and being guided by a sense of practical ethics, we can fulfill our obligations as self-rulers and live up to our responsibilities as Sovereign Individuals.

Self-rule is a prerequisite of self actualization, because it ultimately leads to a state of being in which we are actively reaching our full potential and are living in alignment with our True Will. By understanding ourselves, setting goals, facing challenges, maintaining balance in our lives and making a positive impact in the world, we can achieve self-actualization and fulfill our purpose as Sovereign Individuals.

Let it be known, *The Sovereign Manifesto* is a call to awaken to the truth of our being, to question false narratives and to reject the notion that we are under obligation to, and at the mercy of, those who in no way have our best interest at heart. It is a call to embrace our own Sovereignty, to realize that it is still in our power to break free from the livestock pens of institutional ownership. It is a call to realize one's own authentic nature, and to live accordingly. It is our hope that this manifesto shall inspire you to take control of your own life and to fulfill your unique purpose as a Sovereign Individual.

CHAPTER ONE

"True Will, A Law for All"

The Sovereign Manifesto represents a revolutionary awakening in the realms of social, spiritual, and political enlightenment. It is a call to arms for individuals everywhere to reclaim their power, to discard the shackles of technocratic serfdom, and to embrace the true essence of their being.

The concept of "True Will" is a powerful one, for it speaks to the very core of our existence. It is the innate drive that exists within each and every one of us, the pulsing energy that propels us forward on our journey through life. For too long, this energy has been suppressed, stifled, and repressed by a society that values conformity over individuality. But the time has come for us to rise up and claim our rightful place as the masters of our own fate.

The key to unlocking the full potential of our true will is to be found in the implementation of a new law, one that is all-encompassing and applies to the whole of society. This law shall recognize the sovereignty of the individual.

Without this law, sinister powers will achieve their objective of manufacturing a society under complete technological control, one where the human being is no more than an algorithmic automaton, a barely sentient being whose next purchase can be not only suggested, but *anticipated.*

If they succeed, human beings will be reduced to nothing more than helpless prey, slaves whose minds and bodies are open to molestation and whose life force is vampirized to feed monstrous institutions and entities. If this occurs, then humanity, a once noble creature with God-given, inalienable rights, will be functionally demoted to the level of a lab rat.

This of course must be prevented, at almost any cost. There will be no human future if this downward momentum is allowed to persist. These institutions are not only paving a road to hell, they're setting up toll booths along the way. There must be a new law, one rooted in the spiritual values of human dignity and freedom.

In short, *The Sovereign Manifesto* represents a call to action, a call to break free from the servitude of conformity and to embrace the boundless potential contained in our true nature. It is a call to awaken to the power of our own will, and to use that power to create a better world for ourselves and for future generations.

The True Will of the Individual

The true will is the inner voice that guides us towards the crown of consciousness. It is the path that one is meant to follow, the destiny that one is meant to fulfill. The true will is the key to unlocking our full potential and living a fulfilling life rich with meaning.

The true will is often described as the inner voice that speaks to us from deep within. It is the voice that tells us what we desire and what we are meant to do. It is the voice that speaks to us in the quiet moments, when we are still and contemplative. It is the higher voice that calls to us, guiding us towards a particular star.

One of the key characteristics of the true will is that it is in alignment with our deepest values and beliefs. It is the voice that speaks to us of what truly matters. It is the voice that tells us what we stand for, and what we should fight against.

The true will is not always easy to hear, however. It can be drowned out by the noise and distractions of the world around us. It can be suppressed by our own doubts and fears. To hear the true will, we must learn to quiet the mind, and to listen deeply to our own inner voice.

To follow the true will is not always easy, either. It may require us to make difficult choices, to take risks, and to step out of our comfort zones. It may require us to let go of things that no longer serve us, and to embrace new opportunities. But despite the challenges, following the true will is essential for living a fulfilling life.

When we follow the true will, we are living in alignment with a higher guidance, and with our ultimate purpose. We are living in harmony with the universe and fulfilling our destiny. We are unlocking our full potential and becoming the best version of ourselves.

The Call to Action

We have presented the belief that the true will is the individual's own authentic path. Essential to this noble path is the alignment of the individual's true will with the divine will of their "Sun Within." It is this inner light that holds the key to unlocking one's full potential, while simultaneously contributing to the creation of a more harmonious world.

Now, it's time for action.

We call upon all those who share in this awakened understanding to join us in the pursuit of a better world, a world where the true will of the individual is realigned with the divine will. Together, we can create a world where we're no longer indentured to falsehood, but free to live our true will, and to fulfill the human prophecy of self-actualization.

It has become all too obvious that governments and multinational corporations are pushing for blind obedience and a surrender of personal autonomy. Through policies, mandates, and the weaponization of consumer technologies, they command consensual slavery of the population. Their justifications for this have now moved far outside the bounds of any original ideas about democratic idealism.

It's time to work together towards a common goal. It's time to hear the call. This will require the cultivation of enough respect and understanding among differing individuals to be able to cooperate with each other, to design a world where the individual's better nature can flourish. This represents a new dawn for civilization.

We understand that this is a challenging task, and that it will not happen overnight. It requires the commitment, effort and dedication of all those who choose to join this movement. But we are convinced that together, we can make a difference.

We invite you to take the first step and join us in this journey. You can start by connecting to the **Sun Within**, coming to understand its power and aligning your actions with its will. You can also join a community of like-minded individuals, and share your experiences, knowledge and inspiration. Together, we can create a brighter world for all.

The Importance of Self-Discovery

The process of self-discovery is essential for the Sovereign Individual. It is the key to understanding one's True Will and the role it plays in achieving self-sovereignty.

True Will is the unique purpose or destiny that is inherent to each individual. It is the compass that guides us towards our ultimate goals and aspirations, and it is the foundation upon which self-sovereignty is built.

To discover one's true will, it is necessary to peel back the layers of societal conditioning and external influences that have shaped our beliefs and values. This requires a deep introspection, a willingness to question our assumptions and a commitment to self-exploration. It means being honest with ourselves about our strengths, weaknesses, desires, and fears. It means understanding our place in the world and what we truly want to achieve.

The process of self-discovery is not easy, and it can be uncomfortable at times. It may involve confronting our deepest fears and insecurities, and it may require us to make difficult choices and sacrifices. But it is through this process that we truly come to understand ourselves and our place in the world.

Once we have discovered our Will, it becomes our guiding principle in life. It is the lens through which we view the world, and it shapes our decisions and actions. It is what gives us direction and purpose, and it is what propels us towards self-sovereignty. It is by aligning our actions with our Will that we can truly take control of our lives and become Sovereign Individuals.

Self-discovery is a journey of inner exploration that is essential for the inner development of a Sovereign Individual. It is a process of uncovering one's true self and understanding one's own Will. This process is not only essential for personal growth and fulfillment but also for the ability to live in alignment with one's values and beliefs, free from the influence of external forces.

The process of self-discovery is not a linear one, and it can be divided into several phases.

The first phase is the process of self-awareness, where individuals become aware of their thoughts, emotions, and beliefs and essential values.

The second phase is the process of self-acceptance, where individuals learn to accept and embrace their true selves, including affirming their strengths and recognizing their weaknesses.

The third phase is the process of self-expression, where individuals learn to have the courage to express their true will in their actions and interactions with others.

The final phase is the process of self-actualization, where individuals learn to align their actions and intent with enough concentrated force to fulfill their maximum potential.

Understanding one's own True Will is the ultimate goal of self-discovery. It is the understanding of one's unique purpose and path in life. It is the recognition that each individual is here to fulfill a specific role and that it is their duty to discover and align with this role. By understanding one's own True Will, individuals can live a life of purpose and fulfillment.

Rejecting External Control

The Sovereign Individual recognizes the importance of rejecting external control and manipulation. Society is full of external forces that seek to shape our beliefs, values, and actions. These forces can take many forms, including governments, institutions, corporations, and media. They exert their influence through various means, such as propaganda, censorship, manipulation, and coercion.

The problem with external control is that it undermines our ability to think, act and live independently. It limits our freedom and autonomy, and can cause us to lose connection to our original spirit and essence, in other words, our true will. It can lead us to make decisions that are not in our best interest, even against our best interest, and lead us to live lives that are not at all our own.

To break free from external control, it is necessary to develop a critical and independent mindset. This means learning to question the information and narratives that are presented to us, and to seek out alternative perspectives. It means being willing to challenge the status quo, and to consider different ways of living and thinking.

It is also important to build resilience against manipulation, by understanding the techniques that are being used to influence us and by becoming aware of our own psychological vulnerabilities. We should strive to be aware of our own thoughts and emotions, and to understand how they are being manipulated by external forces.

Breaking free from external control also means taking responsibility for our own lives and actions. It means taking ownership of our thoughts, beliefs, and values, and making conscious choices about how we want to live our lives. It means standing up for what we believe in, and not being afraid to be ourselves.

Consensus trance

Consensus trance refers to the phenomenon where a group of people unconsciously adopt and conform to a set of beliefs, attitudes, and values that are widely held in a society or culture. While consensus trance can provide a sense of unity and social cohesion, it also has several potential dangers, including:

Groupthink: Consensus trance can lead to groupthink, where individuals become so focused on maintaining identification with the dogmas of a group that they ignore potential problems and make poor decisions.

Loss of individuality: When individuals conform to the consensus trance, they may lose their sense of individuality and independence, which can stifle creativity and critical thinking.

Unquestioning obedience: Consensus trance can create an environment where individuals blindly follow the group without questioning its beliefs, values, and attitudes, even if they are harmful or unethical.

Suppression of critique: Consensus trance can lead to the suppression of critique and the rejection of alternative perspectives, which can limit the free exchange of ideas and limit the potential for innovation and progress.

It's important to be aware of the dangers of consensus trance. This can involve questioning commonly held beliefs, seeking out unique perspectives, and actively engaging in critical thinking and self-reflection.

Authority Within

The development of an inner locus of authority is essential for individuals who wish to repudiate external control and live their lives according to their own beliefs and values. It is a process of becoming self-reliant and self-determined, and it requires consistent effort and practice.

The following are five practices that can help an individual to reject external control and develop an inner locus of authority:

1. Sovereign Meditation

Sovereign meditation is the practice of bringing one's attention to the present moment with a sort of detached indifference to what is occurring, withholding judgment in order to observe a situation untinctured by emotion.

This practice is designed to help individuals observe their thoughts and emotions without getting carried away by them. Released from automated, emotional responses, the individual can then turn their attention to challenging any false notions or limiting beliefs that may be holding them back from asserting their full authority.

2. Self-Inquiry

Self-inquiry is the practice of asking oneself questions to gain a deeper understanding of one's thoughts, emotions, and beliefs. This practice helps individuals to identify their own values, beliefs, and desires, and to align their actions with them. Ask yourself deep questions. Good questions to start with are:

> "Who or what, do I believe, represents legitimate authority?"

> "Who or what, do I believe, is the source of wise guidance?"

(If the answer to these two questions is different, take note)

3. Setting Boundaries

Setting boundaries is the practice of communicating and enforcing one's own limits and needs. This practice helps individuals to assert their own authority and to establish healthy relationships with others. Setting boundaries is essential to establishing order in one's kingdom. There must be boundaries for the kingdom to exist, a clear distinction of non-negotiables, in terms of values.

4. Assertiveness Training

Assertiveness training is the practice of learning to express one's own thoughts, feelings, and needs in an honest and direct way. This practice helps individuals to become more confident in expressing themselves and to assert their own authority in various situations. Essentially, this means claiming one's own power of "yes and no."

5. Psychological Self-Defense

Psychological self-defense is the practice of developing the ability to identify, understand and resist manipulation and influence from others. This practice helps individuals to be more aware of the manipulation techniques that others may use on them and to assert their sovereignty by resisting them.

An essential part of psychological self-defense is understanding how dark psychology has infiltrated politics, media, marketing, and even medicine. Trends towards dark psychology have become normalized. Popular music and entertainment no longer hide the fact and proceed to use tactics poisoned with the darkest of intentions. Bit by bit we are trained to tolerate what is essentially intolerable, unethical behavior by predatory characters. As dark psychology infiltrates more and more of our social atmosphere, its target audience gets younger and younger.

The Responsibility of Self-Rule

Self-rule is the state of being in control of one's own life, actions, and decisions. It is the foundation of true sovereignty, and it comes with great responsibilities and obligations. To be a self-ruler is to take ownership of one's life and to actively shape it according to one's own values, goals, and aspirations.

One of the most important responsibilities of self-rule is to take ownership of one's actions and decisions. This means being accountable for the consequences of one's choices, and being willing to acknowledge any negative impact they may have on others. It also means being willing to admit when one has made a mistake and to take steps to make amends.

Another key responsibility of self-rule is to actively shape one's own life according to one's own values and goals. This means being aware of one's own desires and needs, and actively working to achieve them. It also means being willing to take risks and to pursue one's own passions, even if they may not be popular or conventional.

In addition to taking ownership of one's actions and decisions, self-rule also means being aware of one's own limitations and being willing to seek help or guidance when needed. It means having the courage to admit when one is not sure of the best course of action, and the wisdom to consider counsel from others when appropriate.

Self-rule also means being aware of one's own impact on the world around us, and working to make a positive difference. It means being committed to making the world a better place, through acts of service to something greater than the continuance of a hedonistic, base survival.

Rules for Self-Rulers

Know thyself: Understand your own strengths, weaknesses, and motivations.

Avoid disclosing personal information: Keep your cards close to your chest and always maintain a degree of mystery.

Control your emotions: Emotions can cloud judgment and lead to impulsive decisions.

Situational awareness: Keep your eyes and ears open to potential threats or opportunities.

Make time work for you: Grand visions begin as seeds and take time to reach harvest. Be prudent in your use of time. Indecision can become chronic procrastination. Impatience can lead to rash decisions and mistakes.

Maintain a sense of detachment: Remain objective and avoid becoming too invested in any one situation.

Take calculated risks: Carefully weigh the potential benefits against the potential risks before taking action.

Never underestimate your enemies: Always be aware of the capabilities of those who may oppose you.

Be adaptable: Be ready to change course in response to new information or circumstances.

Seek to understand others: Know the motivations and desires of those around you.

Build alliances: Form strategic partnerships to achieve common goals.

Be strategic in your communication: Choose your words carefully to effectively influence and persuade others.

Be a master of disguise: Be able to conceal your feelings and intentions when not in the presence of trusted individuals.

Be persistent: Never give up on your goals, no matter how difficult they may seem. Every obstacle is an opportunity to be greater than circumstance.

Be resourceful: Use your creativity to find solutions when faced with obstacles. Find a way to multiply the effect of limited means.

Avoid showing weakness: Never give others the satisfaction of seeing you falter.

Learn to forgive: Holding grudges will only hold you back. If the matter is small it's often easier to forgive.

Know when to keep a low profile: Avoid drawing unnecessary attention to yourself. Know how to blend into the background when necessary.

Be confident: Believe in yourself and your abilities. Test yourself to determine your actual level of skill, strength and competence. Have confidence, but keep it sensible and aligned with reality.

Learn from your mistakes: Take responsibility for your actions and use them as opportunities to improve.

Be self-reliant: Do not rely on others to achieve your goals. Always be able to rely on yourself.

Always be learning: Constantly seek new knowledge and skills to improve yourself.

CHAPTER TWO

ONE UNDER THE SUN

Spiritual Sovereignty

Humanity suffers from division, that is the heart of most of its problems. But, we are all **one under the sun**. The same sun shines upon every nation, every people, every culture and every creed. It is the connecting path for all life in the solar system. The sun is a symbol for the unity of nature, and the spiritual unity of mankind.

It is the Sun that is the source of all life and energy in the solar system and it is the sun that holds the key to humanity understanding its purpose and place in the world.

The true will of the individual is the path of the sun, the destiny that one is meant to fulfill. It is simultaneously the calling that comes from deep within, the inner voice that guides us towards the light of our own particular star. By aligning our will with the gravity of this star, we unlock our higher potential.

The sun is the benevolent symbol of power, energy, and authority, the driving force and guiding principle behind all living things. By connecting our consciousness to this power we connect to the source of all life and energy, and we become a part of its great cosmic cycle of birth, life, and rebirth.

History shows that the civilizations who aligned their will with this cosmic power (by its many names and forms) have sustained the most enduring empires. Solar religions had far more to do with an individual's interface and harmony with the natural world, than the disagreements over doctrine that have fueled the religious wars since then.

In those days no one ever questioned whether God existed, because God arose each day. The question of whether God was dead, or would resurrect, on the other hand, was a living drama acted out yearly in the changing of the seasons.

Would the Sun return after the long expanse of a brutally cold and harsh winter? Would the divine light return to renew the life of earth? These are the original questions of religion, the bedrock of spirituality.

Spirituality is the act of consciousness looking into a frightening darkness while affirming a triumphant light. It is this conscious affirmation of light that represents the human contribution to the sun's return.

We call upon all those who share in the vision of a new dawn to join us in the pursuit of a brighter world, a world where the thoughts, words and deeds of the individual once again reflect a higher truth.

We are approaching the endgame of a long-fought battle, one where loss will mean not only a total subjugation of the population, but the end of humanity as we know it.

Yet a potential victory still exists, a victory which includes the liberation of the human spirit from limitations that it has been conditioned to accept as unconditional.

The Sovereign Manifesto is for those who are no longer willing to surrender their life force to parasitic influences. This includes the influence of those dark magicians who manipulate the social contract to control and coerce a demoralized population into its own surrender.

It is time to recognize and honor those eternal principles that rule forever, and are embodied in the Sun. It is time for all with courage and strength to stand and defend the integrities of life and light by affirming their Divine Right.

Buddha, Christ and Odin:
Exemplars of Sovereign Consciousness

The connection between sovereign consciousness, Buddha Consciousness, Christ Consciousness, and Odinic Consciousness is rooted in the understanding that true spiritual attainment is the realization of one's own inherent power and authority.

In ancient mythologies, we see examples of figures who embody this realization of self-sovereignty. The Buddha, for example, is said to have attained enlightenment through the understanding of the Four Noble Truths and the Eightfold Path. This enlightenment, or Buddha Consciousness, is the attainment of a state of understanding and mastery over one's own mind and actions.

Similarly, in the Christian tradition, Christ, "the light of the world" is seen as the embodiment of God made flesh. The name Christ, from the Greek *khristos*, means "the anointed" and refers to chrism, a sacred oil used to ritually initiate sacred rulers.

> In relation to the power and authority of the individual, Christ spoke: "is it not written in your law, ye are gods?"

Through his teachings and ultimate sacrifice, the story of Christ represents the realization of sovereignty and spiritual consciousness. Establishing himself as the Sun of God, he encouraged his followers to see themselves as children of God, so that they could ultimately come to understand their own divinity and power.

In Norse mythology, Odin, the All-father, is known for his wisdom and knowledge. Through sacrifice, he hung from the world tree, Yggdrasil, for nine days, to gain wisdom and power. He is an embodiment of the idea that true spiritual attainment is often achieved through sacrifice and self-discovery.

These mythological figures demonstrate that sovereignty and spiritual consciousness are intimately connected. True spiritual attainment is not just about transcendence and detachment from the material world, but about understanding and embracing one's own power and authority. It's about understanding that we all contain the seed of the divine. Some just put more work into cultivating it.

In this respect, sovereign consciousness, Buddha Consciousness, Christ Consciousness, and Odinic consciousness are all different expressions of the same idea that spiritual attainment is the realization of one's own inherent power and authority. Through understanding and embracing our own sovereignty, we can attain true spiritual enlightenment by cultivating a life rich with individual meaning.

Sovereignty, Spirituality and the Sun

Sovereignty and spirituality are two concepts that have been intertwined throughout human history. The idea of a sovereign individual or nation, is closely linked to the concept of a higher connecting power or divine authority. In many ancient cultures, the sun was seen as a powerful symbol of sovereignty and spiritual power and revered as a symbol of benevolent and rightful authority.

Sun gods were seen as sovereigns of the heavenly spheres, linking the Sun to the idea of divinity and spiritual power. Just as the Sun brings life and fertility back to the earth after winter, so too does it bring inspiration and enlightenment back to humanity after a dark age.

The sun has long been a powerful symbol of the divine, and was often associated with the synthesis of social, political and spiritual responsibilities held as sovereign power under the title of Sacred Kingship. The heads of this sacred fraternity are recorded in ancient temples as the "king's list."

It was this ancient institution, or sacred fraternity that held responsibility for spiritually shepherding and wisely guiding civilization from the earliest dawn of human consciousness.

Although it would still take many centuries before the memories of divine law would fade enough for politicians to operate independent of its legacy, without a sovereign protector the majesty of civilization began to wane.

With the end of sacred rule, the teachings and leadership of this ancient fraternity began to fade into the realm of the occult. From this point forward, humanity would become prey to vicious tyrants and brutal conquest. No longer guided by higher principles, usurpers dominated what was once a sacred office. Driven by base ambitions, glorious nations were destroyed by private greed and excess. Whole populations were led astray by one demagogue after another, one high ranking minister after another, or one ambitious senator after another until the echoes of sovereignty's original greatness had faded into the realms of either scripture or myth.

In ancient times, the sun was often seen not only as the source of all power and authority, but also as the power which brings prosperity and abundance to the whole of the earth.

In ancient cultures, the sun was consistently associated with wise rulers, individuals who were born to be representatives of the sun on earth. They were held to be chosen by the sun to govern and rule, and they held a special relationship with the sun, which gave them the power and authority to govern.

Sovereignty, spirituality, and the sun are all interconnected concepts that form the foundation of a re-dawning spiritual movement.

At its core, this movement is about reclaiming one's personal power and autonomy, both as an individual and as a member of a sovereign nation. It is about recognizing the divine right and responsibility of each person to govern themselves, and to live in accordance with a sense of cosmic balance. This movement is also about connecting with the spiritual power of the sun, which symbolizes the energy, light, and vitality that is available to all of us when we tap into our own inner power.

This movement is about the power of the individual, and the Divine Right that each holds over their own lives, as gifted to them by the Sovereign Sun. It is about recognizing that true freedom and autonomy can only be achieved when we take responsibility for our own actions, and make choices that align with a higher will. This is not about conforming to societal norms or expectations, but about living in accordance with our own inner guidance and wisdom.

The sun represents the light of truth and understanding, as well as the warmth of compassion and love. It is a symbol of our connection to the divine, and of the power that is available to us when we align our will with the natural rhythms and cycles of the universe.

A spiritual movement based on the symbol of the Sovereign Sun could help to create a more harmonious world in a number of ways. Here are just a few examples:

1. Emphasis on Individual Responsibility

By aligning the true will of the individual with the divine will of the sun, the movement would encourage individuals to take responsibility for their actions and to strive for personal growth and self-improvement. This could lead to a more harmonious world, as individuals would be more likely to act in ways that are positive and beneficial to themselves and others.

2. Connection to Nature

The movement would promote a connection to the natural world and the power of the sun. By understanding the importance of the sun, and the role it plays in the natural world, individuals would be more likely to respect and care for the environment. This could lead to a more sustainable and harmonious world.

3. Encouragement of Understanding and Acceptance

By promoting the idea that everyone's true will is connected to the divine will of the sun, the movement would encourage individuals to accept and respect the unique paths and destinies of others. This could lead to a more harmonious world, as people would be more likely to coexist in peace and understanding.

4. Emphasis on Personal Growth

The movement would encourage individuals to strive for personal growth and self-improvement. By aligning their true will with the divine will of the sun, individuals would be more likely to reach their full potential and to make positive contributions to the world. This could lead to a more harmonious and prosperous world for all.

The Divine Will of the Sun

The sun has been revered as a symbol of power, energy, and life since ancient times and worshiped as a deity in many cultures throughout history. Its power and importance have been acknowledged by almost every enduring civilization.

In ancient Egypt, the sun god Ra was considered the ruler of the world, and his daily journey across the sky was seen as a symbol of the cycle of birth, life, and rebirth. In ancient Greece, the sun god Helios was believed to be the ruler of the heavens, and his chariot was seen as a symbol of the sun's daily journey across the sky.

The Inca civilization of South America had a strong belief in the sun god Inti, who was considered the ancestor of the Inca people and the most powerful deity in their pantheon. The Inca emperor was believed to be the son of Inti and held a special relationship with the sun god.

The ancient Chinese believed that the sun was controlled by the god Shangdi, who was considered the ruler of the heavens. They built temples to honor the sun, including the Temple of the Sun in Beijing, built during the Ming Dynasty.

The Mayan civilization of Central America also had a strong belief in the power of the sun. The Mayans believed that the sun was controlled by the god Kinich Ahau.

Many Mayan pyramids, such as the Temple of the Sun in Palenque, were built to honor the sun god.

The Roman cult of Mithras was a mystery religion that was popular among soldiers and merchants in the Roman Empire. The cult was based on the worship of the god Mithras, who was associated with the sun. Mithras was believed to be the bringer of light and truth and the savior of humanity. The cult of Mithras was particularly popular among the Roman military, and many Mithraic temples have been found in Roman military camps.

The Roman Empire also had a cult of Sol Invictus, which means "the Unconquered Sun." This cult was initiated by Emperor Aurelian in 274 CE and was focused on the worship of the sun as a deity. Sol Invictus was considered to be a powerful and benevolent deity and his cult was popular among the Roman elite.

In Christianity, the sun has been used as a symbol of Jesus Christ, who is often referred to as the "light of the world." The Bible also contains many references to the sun, such as in the book of Malachi, where it is written that "the Sun of Righteousness will rise with healing in his wings."

As the ultimate source of light and life, the sun has long-held the spiritual key to understanding our purpose and place in the world. The sun has been the basis of countless religions spanning across millennia all the way back to the earliest primordial dawn. Mighty empires have come and gone over those millennia yet the sun god still lives on, shining to this day.

The sun is the driving force behind all living things, including the individual's consciousness. It's time for this understanding to be as innate and obvious to us today, as it was to our oldest ancestors.

The Alignment of Will

The alignment of the will of the individual with the divine will of the **Sun Within**, is the key to unlocking our human potential. It is the path to understanding our purpose and our place in the solar system. By connecting to the Sun Within, and understanding its power, we become co-creators of a new dawn.

The true will is the inner voice that guides us towards this light. Guided by this light, the divine will gives our will its direction.

This alignment is not a one-time event, it's an ongoing process. It requires a constant effort to stay connected and to align our will and our actions with this higher principle. It's not an easy task but it's worth the effort.

The benefits of this type of psychological alignment are numerous, including increased self-awareness, self-knowledge, and a deepening sense of meaning and purpose.

Cultivating psychological health in a society is essential. The sun, as a symbol used by the renowned psychologist, Carl Jung, itself represents psychological health and its meaning in dream symbolism is closely linked to individual wholeness.

At a societal level, a culture of wholeness would be one where responsible individuals can live in harmony with their natural drives and in alignment with the natural order of the universe. Does this mean there will be no conflict? Of course not, life will continue to be life, but unlike present circumstances, it will be the kind of life that can be sustained for millennia to come.

Sovereignty, True Will and Divine Right

These ancient, interconnected concepts are deeply rooted in our civilization, in both the political and spiritual spheres. Together, they form the foundation of a society in which responsible individuals are largely free to govern themselves and live in accordance with their own beliefs and values.

At its core, Sovereignty is the idea that a nation or a people have the right to self-rule, free from external control or influence. It is the belief that a country's power and authority should come from within, rather than being imposed from without. This concept is closely tied to the idea of the Divine Right of the

Individual, which holds that every person has an inherent and natural right to govern themselves. Together, these concepts form the foundation of a society in which individuals have the freedom and autonomy to make their own decisions.

The concept of True Will is also closely tied to Sovereignty and the Divine Right of the Individual. True Will refers to the inherent drive or purpose that each person has within themselves. It is the idea that every individual has a unique path or destiny that they are meant to follow, and that this path is in alignment with the greater good of the universe. By living in accordance with their True Will, individuals are able to tap into their own inner power and potential, and contribute to the greater good of society as a whole.

In a society that is based on the principles of Sovereignty, True Will, and the Divine Right, individuals are free to govern themselves and live in accordance with their own beliefs and values. This can lead to a more just and equitable society, as well as a greater sense of community and shared identity among its citizens. Additionally, by living in accordance with their True Will, individuals are able to tap into their own inner power and potential, and contribute to the greater good of society as a whole.

The connection between Sovereignty, True Will, and the Divine Right of the Individual is not just political in nature, but also spiritual. These concepts are deeply rooted in the belief that each individual has a unique purpose and destiny, and that by living in accordance with this purpose, they are able to tap into their own inner power and potential. This idea is not only empowering for the individual, but it also contributes to the greater good of society as a whole.

CHAPTER THREE

The Sovereign Process

Self-Actualization and Individuation

Self-actualization is the realization of one's full potential, the attainment of the highest level of individual growth and development. In psychological terms, it is the ultimate goal of human existence and the ultimate expression of human potential. It is the process of becoming fully and authentically who we are meant to be, of living in alignment with our deepest values and highest aspirations.

Individuation, on the other hand, is the psychological process of becoming an individual, of differentiating oneself from others and the collective unconscious. It is the process of integrating the psyche, of becoming whole and complete.

Together, self-actualization and individuation represent the attainment of full expression and autonomy. By breaking free from the bonds of the mundane and the transitory, and developing a connection to the mythic and timeless, it is possible to transcend the social limitations of our persona to connect with a sense of self beyond all masks.

In bold language, the journey of self-actualization and individuation represents the ultimate human attainment, the realization of our true potential as spiritual beings having a human experience. It is the process of breaking free from the cramped eggshell of a limiting model of the world and divorcing ourselves from the burdens of the collective unconscious and its murky swamp of mass psychosis.

> Self-actualization represents a mountain peak attainment, in terms of human experience.

Individuation, on the other hand, is more about knowing which individual mountain peak is yours to climb, that summit which is unique to your individual destiny.

The Path to Self-Actualization

The journey of self-discovery and self-rule ultimately leads to the state of self-actualization, a state of being in which an individual is enjoying near maximum potential and is living with alignment, and without internal conflict. Self-actualization is the ultimate goal of the Sovereign Individual, a state of fulfillment, spiritual contentment, and purpose.

The path to self-actualization begins with self-discovery. By understanding ourselves and our True Will, we are able to make conscious choices and take control of our own lives. We can set goals and create a plan of action that will help us achieve our purpose.

As we work towards self-actualization, we will encounter obstacles and challenges. These will test our resolve and our ability to remain true to our Will. These challenges are opportunities for growth and they will make us stronger.

In order to reach self-actualization, it's also important to maintain a balance between our physical, mental, emotional, and spiritual well-being. A healthy body and mind are essential for the journey of self-discovery and self-rule. We must take care of ourselves, by eating well, getting enough rest, exercising and engaging in activities that bring a sense of fulfillment.

Self-actualization also involves a deep understanding of our place in the world and our role in the greater community. As Sovereign Individuals, we must strive to make a positive impact in the world.

> The journey of self-discovery and self-rule ultimately leads to the state of self-actualization.

By understanding ourselves, setting goals, facing challenges, maintaining balance in our lives we can achieve self-actualization and fulfill our purpose as Sovereign Individuals.

How to Self-Actualize

Self-actualization is a lifelong process of becoming the best version of oneself. It involves understanding and embracing one's true potential, and working towards fulfilling that potential. The exact steps for achieving self-actualization will vary for each individual, but some common practices and exercises that can be used to help in this process include:

Self-Reflection

This is the process of taking time to reflect on one's inner world. This can be accomplished most efficiently through writing and introspection. This step helps individuals to gain a deeper understanding of themselves and their values, which is essential for self-actualization.

Setting Goals

Setting clear, meaningful, and achievable goals is essential for self-actualization. This helps individuals to focus on what they want to achieve and to take action towards achieving it.

Eliminating Limiting Beliefs

Limiting beliefs are negative thoughts or beliefs that hold individuals back from achieving their goals. These beliefs often stem from past experiences or societal norms. Identifying and eliminating limiting beliefs is an important step in achieving self-actualization.

Building Self-Awareness

Building self-awareness means becoming more aware of one's thoughts, feelings, and behaviors, and how they affect one's life. This can be done through various practices, including art, meditation and hypnotherapy. Combine all three for a powerful cocktail.

Embracing Change

Self-actualization requires individuals to be open to change and to be willing to step out of their comfort zones. This means being willing to try new things, to take risks, and to learn from mistakes.

Taking Action

It's important to take action towards achieving self-actualization. This means setting goals, making plans, and taking steps towards achieving them. This step requires individuals to be committed and persistent in their pursuit of self-actualization.

Divine Right and the Sovereign Sun

The concept of Sovereign Spirituality is rooted in the belief that each individual is an inherently connected being, "one under the Sun" with their own unique purpose or True Will.

This belief is closely tied to the idea of Divine Right, which states that individuals possess a natural and inalienable authority to govern their own lives, free from external manipulation and control.

Together, these concepts form the foundation of the Sovereign Individual, who recognizes and exercises their Divine Right to rule over their own cosmos and be guided by their own compass.

The deeper implications of solar spirituality suggest the idea that each individual is a microcosm of the larger cosmic universe. Through this connection it is within their ability to tap into the same universal energy and consciousness that created the cosmos. This connection is identical to the individual's "genius," or inner spark.

Divine Right is the right and authority to govern one's own life. Slaves and subjects are controlled by external forces.

How many of those born as slaves are capable of becoming autonomous and self-governing beings? How many would feel naked without shackles?

In exercising their Divine Right, Individuals are clothed in the robes of responsibility. For a Self-Ruler, responsibility and power sit upon level scales, one must not outweigh the other. We must never take responsibility for that which we have no power over, and we can never wield a power without an equivalent amount of responsibility.

The Sovereign Individual is one who recognizes and exercises their Divine Right. As a Sovereign Individual, one takes full responsibility for and assumes power over the kingdom of their own conscious existence.

The Curriculum: Sovereignty 101

The Curriculum is a suggested study course for understanding the role and responsibilities of a Sovereign. This Curriculum represents a self-education aimed at developing the skills and characteristics necessary for an individual to lead themselves and others.

Subjects of Study for Self-Rulers
---

1. Leadership: The ability to inspire and guide others to work towards a common goal.

2. Strategic thinking: The ability to plan and make decisions that will benefit the kingdom in the long term.

3. Diplomacy: The ability to negotiate and maintain good relationships with other leaders and nations.

4. Military strategy: The ability to plan and lead military campaigns to protect the kingdom.

5. Economic management: The ability to manage the kingdom's resources and economy.

6. Justice and fairness: The ability to make fair and just decisions, and to ensure that the laws of the kingdom are upheld.

7. Visionary thinking: The ability to see beyond the present and to anticipate future challenges and opportunities.

8. Empathy: The ability to understand and relate to the needs and concerns of the people.

9. Resilience: The ability to handle stress and adapt to changing circumstances.

10. Communication: The ability to effectively convey ideas and information to others.

11. Cultural understanding: The ability to understand and appreciate the cultural diversity within the kingdom.

12. Emotional intelligence: The ability to understand and manage one's emotions and the emotions of others.

13. Wisdom: The ability to make sound judgments and decisions based on knowledge, experience and insight.

14. Self-control: The ability to control one's impulses and emotions.

15. Integrity: The ability to act in accordance with moral principles, and to be honest and trustworthy.

16. Courage: The ability to face difficult challenges and to make difficult decisions.

17. Creativity: The ability to think outside the box and to come up with new and innovative ideas.

18. Intelligence: The ability to think critically and to understand complex information and issues.

19. Decision-making: The ability to make decisions quickly and effectively.

20. Divine Right: Developing a spiritual connection with an inner Authority or "higher principal" operating within the Individual's own consciousness. It is from this place that the voice of an inner authority can be heard. Sovereignty is a blood pact with God.

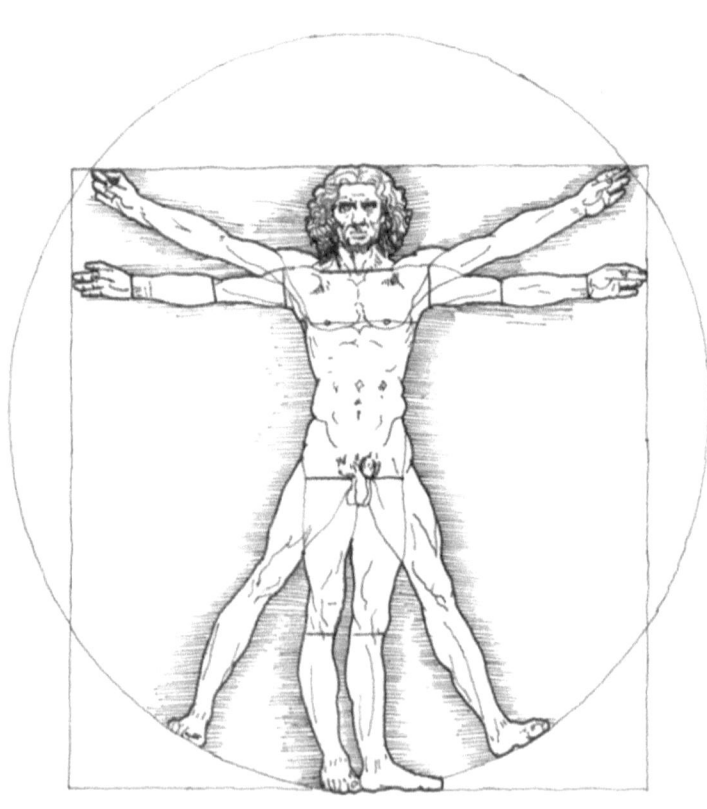

CHAPTER FOUR

Sovereign Politick

A Legitimate Critique

Sovereignty is the keystone that unites the arches of millennia-spanning civilizations together. It is the foundation upon which legitimate authority is built, the source of all rights.

Without sovereignty, there can be no rights, no law, and no order. In its absence, chaos reigns supreme, and the result is a fragmented society.

The source of sovereignty is the source of rights, and the origin of that source has always been in a transcendent principle, in other words, God or the Gods.

Without God, there can be no sovereignty, and without sovereignty, there is no legitimizing force. Without legitimacy, there is no law, and without law, there is no order. It is a delicate balance that must be maintained to ensure the survival of society.

But who or what is this God that grants the scepter of sovereignty? This is a question that has been pondered by philosophers and theologians for centuries. Some believe that God is an all-powerful, all-knowing creator, while others believe that God is simply a representation of the natural order of the universe.

For most of human history, the sun was the central symbol for the divine, of the bond between heaven and earth. It was this bond that the sovereign's life represented.

> As the source of natural law which governs the world, the sun was understood to also be the source of divine law for guiding mankind.

This law was reflected in the concept of sovereignty and divine right, also known as the mandate of heaven. Regardless of one's personal beliefs, it is clear that without God or Gods, there can be no sovereignty, and without sovereignty, there can be no order.

In chaos, all is fractured into disorganized fractals colliding with one another for supremacy. It is a place where evil can go unchecked and good cannot long survive.

Sovereignty is characterized by its concentration of power, and it is through this concentration of power that order is maintained and chaos is kept at bay.

Sovereignty is the foundation upon which society is built. It is the source of rights and the legitimizing force that keeps chaos chained. It is a concept that has been central to human societies for centuries, and it is a reminder that without order, all is given to chaos, and in chaos, entire civilizations collapse. Sovereignty is the source of our rights and the God that is the source of all things good.

Sovereignty, as defined by *The Sovereign Manifesto*, is a declaration of independence from subjugation, a state of possessing the exclusive deed of ownership, in regards to oneself.

This is a reminder that life, liberty, and the pursuit of happiness are inalienable rights gifted to mankind by the Sovereign Sun, or "God." This understanding of sovereignty is rooted in the belief that mankind's life is not meant to be divorced from a higher purpose.

Contemporary thought often seeks to separate mankind's existence from any kind of spiritual or divine purpose. However, this line of thinking also abrogates the ancient rule of law from its legitimate basis. The inalienable rights that governments hold hostage are not the possession of external organizations - they are mankind's birthright. It is the awareness of this truth that all true religions seek to provoke.

In seeking to abolish ancient monarchical traditions, ambitious politicians established a rule by the mob. This mob form of government, far less noble in its disposition and far more numerous in its conflicting elements, has since given rise to a carousel of demagogic politicians.

In this descent from sacred origins to pure Machiavellian deceit, leadership changed in both form and function. Rather than having kings and queens act as the symbolic father and mother of a nation, politicians assumed the role of mediator between the people and their inheritance. Divorced from its sacred origins, politics became an arena for criminal indulgence.

> Without a legitimate integrity, power promotes its self-interest at the expense of all.

Without the traditional stability and legitimacy that came with an inherited monarchical title, this new class of pure politicians had to keep the masses continuously enthralled with a never ending political drama, performing on stage as saviors and scoundrels, summoning the hopes and fears of the masses with an almost evangelical touch.

With the King's head now in a basket, there was no longer a sovereign protector, which meant that whole nations and their populations became subject to the self interest of those who were positioned to fill the power void: a coalition of bankers, industrialists and armament suppliers.

Nations were now to be controlled by economic means, destroyed through well funded wars and then rebuilt in such a way that their former glory could be buried under mountains of interest from enormous debts.

Like black magicians, politicians learned how to stir the adolescent emotions of the population in a cauldron of confusion, brewing a poisonous concoction of political resentments and social frustrations that could be released, like a weapon, upon political opponents.

Despite the noble ideas embodied in the American revolutionary myth, in declaring independence from the English King, ownership to a new order of government, one to be controlled by financiers, was conceived.

The Sovereign Manifesto reminds us that true sovereignty is not found in external organizations or governments, but rather in the recognition of the inalienable rights gifted to us by a higher power. It calls for a return to the understanding that our lives have a divine purpose and that true freedom can only be found when we are in alignment with that purpose.

The Sovereign Manifesto serves as a reminder of the importance of divinity in the concept of sovereignty. It reminds us that true sovereignty is not something that can be granted or taken away by external forces, but rather it is a birthright gifted to us by the Divine. It is a call to reclaim our inalienable rights, and to live our lives in alignment with the higher purpose, to which we are all connected.

> "We hold these truths to be self-evident..."

These powerful words, written at the founding of a new nation, speak to the idea that certain truths are so obvious that they need not be proven or justified. But what does this say about the nature of truth and the self in relation to it?

Is self-evidence the only requirement for legitimizing a new law, and for creating a new form of government?

Is a self-evident truth all that's required to lay the foundation stone for a new nation?

These are questions that have been pondered for centuries, and they call into question the very foundations of our legal and political assumptions.

If truth is self-evident, then truth must simultaneously be a part of oneself and a reflection of something higher. This higher power, whatever we call it, is the source of our inalienable rights. All law, therefore, must be rooted in a transcendent function, as there can be no legitimacy in a law that separates itself from its higher legitimizing principle.

The only *legitimate* purpose of the sovereign state is to serve and protect the sovereign rights of the individuals who comprise that state. That is its only mission, it's Holy Mission. The sovereign state must have no other function, and so the very existence of the sovereign state must be defined by, and its power constrained to, this jurisdiction.

We hold these truths to be self-evident, that mankind is equally endowed with inalienable rights *by its creator*. This understanding of sovereignty and inalienable rights is not only the foundation of a free and just society, but it is also a reminder of our connection to something greater than ourselves.

Neglected Centuries

For centuries, sovereignty has been a key concept in political and legal discourse. At its core, sovereignty represents the power and function of governing.

Originating in France in the late 16th century, the concept of sovereignty has undergone various interpretations and adaptations in different political and intellectual contexts.

Sovereignty, like the sun, represents an orientation toward something "fixed." It is the same principle that is the source of all true law. Without a fixed point, any change creates disorientation. Without a fixed point, a society suffers cultural and social disorientation. That fixed point might be: a temple, a mountain, a relic, an altar, a throne, an inspired leader, a black rock or a holy book.

In ancient mythology, this power has often been associated with kings and pharaohs. These individuals, revered as incarnations of the sun, and stewards of divine order represented the source of orientation and authority for entire nations.

There have been great debates about the legitimacy and shape of government, with questions about who holds sovereignty and whether it represents abstract or concrete authority, whether it belongs to an individual or a collective, and whether its position and exercise must be in the same hands or can be separate.

In today's ever-changing political landscape, the question continually arises: does sovereignty still have a role to play?

As we navigate through different interpretations and competing ideas, one thing remains clear: the concept of sovereignty holds a timeless and enduring significance in our understanding of power and governance. The connection between the sun and sovereignty, present in ancient monarchical forms of government serves as a reminder of the enduring power and authority that sovereignty represents.

The communist revolution began by questioning the very nature of sovereign rights and authority, but ended with those same revolutionaries appropriating sovereign rights and powers. This included assuming complete authority to: create laws, enforce them with punishments, change laws, mint currency, impose taxes, and declare war.

Because of the inherent lack of legitimacy in their efforts, those who manipulate the systems of contemporary governments, must invent new, ever more abstract concepts to both confuse and transition a naive public's shaky acceptance of their unconstitutional measures from initial outrage into an unquestioned presupposition bolstered by "social proof." From this presupposition, those in power are able to decree "what will be" to those who would be ruled.

> Without the actual object of sovereignty, there is no legitimate power.

This is why, in many cases, what is mistaken for "authority" is nothing more than a hired actor playing a role. In this political theater, citizens are constrained by law to kneel to the policies of great criminals as if they were great kings.

The concept of sovereignty is a complex and ever-evolving one, and its object is essential for the legitimacy of any form of governance.

Demo-crazy

The origins of democracy can be traced back to the ancient world, where the Athenians developed the concept of direct democracy. This system allowed citizens to vote on laws and policies directly, rather than through elected representatives.

Even at this stage, democracy faced numerous criticisms and challenges. Many philosophers, including Plato and Aristotle, have pointed out the weaknesses of democracy, such as the potential for mob rule and the fact that it can lead to the rise of demagogues.

The revolutionary wars of the 18th and 19th centuries brought democracy to the forefront of political discourse. These revolutions, such as the American Revolution and the French Revolution, aimed to overthrow existing systems of governance and establish democratic systems. However, the social repercussions of these revolutions were significant, including the Reign of Terror in France which was a period of unimaginable public violence and mass killings unthinkable before the age of revolution.

Democratic revolution holds a special place in the public imagination, but as a model form of governance, it is not without its tragic flaws. It is important to acknowledge its weaknesses, and to be aware of the potential social repercussions of democratic revolutions.

Sovereignty, at each step in its descent, has lost elements of its original meaning. With progressive deterioration, we have arrived where we are today. What we call government today is a contradiction of earlier established concepts of law and state. Through intensive efforts to blur the definition of sovereignty, each new generation suffers a further distortion in its understanding of legitimate authority.

This mutilation of sovereignty has fostered a feeding ground for opportunists to tear off bites from its original body of rights and dignities, until nothing remains of its crown except the dent in the ground where it fell.

Today, the European Union, with its claims of power over national decisions, has sought to undermine the notion of sovereignty itself.

In the new conception, sovereignty does not refer to an actual object, but operates in the assumptive realm of imagination and ideas.

Can "the right to rule" really be assumed from the realm of imagination and ideas?

What magic turns a man's handwriting into an enforceable law? What letters spell words powerful enough to govern hundreds of millions of people over the course of centuries? What authority gives its authenticating stamp to the official documents of a new nation?

Could the cornerstone of a new nation's entire political structure really rest on a piece of animal-skin parchment, scribbled with words by the hand of a man endowed with a belief in his own God-given right of self-determination, as is the case with the American Declaration of Independence?

Who can explain the power of ink and quill to dissolve the legitimacy of an established empire with one stroke while laying the cornerstone for a new nation with the next?

If what that famous hand wrote was true and "all men are," indeed, "created equal," then could not that same right of self-determination be equally in your own hands?

The Legitimizing Ritual

The phrase "all men are created equal" is a great one-liner, and it became the legal justification for the legitimizing of a new nation.

On one hand, it was an every man's phrase, aimed at winning approval from those who might question the new nation's basis for legitimate authority. On the other hand, it was intended to confront the legal reality of the time, which was that the authority to make official laws or form a nation required the authenticating signature of a sovereign king.

Thomas Jefferson was not a king, but with ink and pen and animal skin he conceived verses powerful enough to make him equal to a king, at which point he then proceeded to write the declaration of independence for a new nation over which he would later preside.

The scene just described represents the core 'legitimizing ritual' of American power structure.

We are made to suppose that this ritual was sanctioned by a higher power, that this piece of writing represents a legally justified claim on all territory, resources and lives of the people occupying a great stretch of the North American continent.

If not a higher power, then who really writes the script for a nation's "manifest destiny?"

Was it from Jefferson's own mind, and from Jefferson's own hand that came this seemingly magical script of letters that spelled words powerful enough to appropriate what was previously held only by a King?

In beautiful calligraphy, the right to make laws, enforce punishments, impose capital punishment, mint currency, impose taxes, and declare war, was transferred from a King to "We the People."

The word authority is closely linked, in its etymological origins, to the word *author*. The founding fathers are considered sacrosanct in the American myth because they're considered "creator gods," authorities of a new political conception—one that became not only a new belief, but a new covenant of law.

In 1776, by flickering lamplight, revolutionary documents were composed that brought sublime ideas and self-evident truths into the light of consciousness for all to see. By dipping thoughts in ink and putting them to parchment, the course of history was shifted and the fate of empires forever altered.

The writing of the Declaration of Independence represented a criminal act according to the laws of that time. The founding fathers were first outlaws, then lawgivers.

Some believe the war for independence was actually a political coup brokered by self-interest and financed by foreign banks, like many wars since the fall of monarchy. The colonists may have won freedom from a one percent tax on tea, but it came at the cost of becoming a tax base for an organization of bankers, investors, and enterprising industrialists.

In this newly formed republic, politicians would become the bankers of sovereignty, positioned to hold the rights and securities of "the People." For this service, fees and interest could gradually nibble away the sovereign rights and wealth of a population viewed as no more than livestock.

Despite what might have begun with good and sincere intentions, this fictive, unitary sovereign concept framed as "We the People" has no actual legal reality.

Who is the 'we' who *actually holds* this power? If no one knows who actually holds the power, then who is accountable for governmental misconduct? A system of power divorced from accountability easily becomes a playground for criminals.

A government of 'We the People,' can be held to no account for its crimes because the identity of the actual perpetrators is easily concealed beneath the smudged fingerprints of the multitude. After all, it's what the *voters* wanted.

In the American democratic system, accumulating guilt for national crimes is partly resolved through the ritual sacrifice of political scapegoats. Like the Roman circus maximus, democratic elections are a spectacle of chariot races to rally hoorays and boos from intoxicated plebs.

Such a diverse group, as popular democracy claims to represent, is merely a collection of fragmentary groups with the self-interest of each set one against the other in constant political battle.

Sovereign Power

In the beginning, the words sovereign and sovereignty were used to characterize concrete phenomena of significant heights such as mountains or towers. They were also used to describe the power of God.

Even after the reference to physical objects was lost, the application to God continued for much longer. In terms of rule, sovereignty described the highest final decision-making authority. Those who had no earthly lord above them in regard to such a power and were not dependent on the consent of others were called sovereign.

Throughout history, objects of power such as crowns have been symbols of sovereignty. The Crown, itself

literally the gold rays of the sun linking earth with heaven, symbolizes the sovereign's link with God. The legitimate power to rule came not from below, but from above.

The power to govern was always held by *an Individual* who exercised it. Sovereignty was not merely based on the use of instruments of power, but on the highest independent power of disposition. Those who ultimately remained masters of their exercise of power were sovereign.

Historically, sovereignty recognized the social order as established by God-given or natural law. This has been true since the earliest establishment of law and order in civilization. As a result, sovereignty can never be legitimately subsumed by any artifice, any contemporary social contract.

The sovereign's duty has always been to implement this God-given natural law or reestablish it when it was violated. This was the ancient Egyptian concept of Ma'at.

The Question of Legitimacy

Since the last days of the pharaohs, there has been the recurring question of legitimacy. It was a problem for the Hebrews after Moses, a problem for the Greeks after Alexander, and a problem for the Romans after Caesar.

In more modern times, the growing epitaph of victims from various political revolutions, world wars and humanitarian interventions is a constant reminder of the consequences that can occur in the absence of legitimate authority.

Capitalizing on the generational confusion surrounding legitimate authority, entrenched banking systems move to spawn artificial governments. These artificial governments possess no concrete object of sovereignty.

Instead, their principle of power works through abstract and fictitious entities, whether a democratic "we the people" a "communist party" or more recently, "a community" of people loosely associated through preconstructed social identities, or even sexual fetishes.

With no actual sovereignty held as a security, the artifice of the state must be temporarily animated with personalities in the form of controllable dictators brought to power by well financed coups or sub-autonomous politicians elected by seemingly "democratic" means.

Like a bank, government is a transactionary institution that manages the delicate balance between the rights and powers of the people and their actual use.

Public authority, much like a trust fund, must be entrusted to the capable hands of representatives of the people, a trustee or guardian of the trust. But, how much trust does it take to let a con-artist *hold your inheritance*?

The legal difficulties around the legitimate transfer of sovereignty "to the people," who technically cannot exercise this power themselves, is said to have been resolved by the constitution, *a revered document* that serves as the ultimate authority.

But one must ask, what authority was in the hand that wrote this document? How is it possible to *channel* the authority to legitimately authorize a massive transference of power from one party to another?

Who or what grants a particular individual's hand the power to do so? For millennia, the answer to this question was: only the hand of a King.

In the midst of late medieval religious schisms, politicians emerged as a powerful influence. Like the branch of an invasive vine grafted onto the root of an ancient tree, politicians positioned themselves to reap the fruits of authority. Moving away from the notions of religious truth, theirs was a focus on pure political power. This opened the door for Machiavelli's revised template on how to rule, as described in "The Prince." From this point forward, sacred rulership steadily devolved into the amoral game of political cunning that it is today.

Although politicians continue to borrow and use powerful ideas, images and symbols from the past it is not because they actually possess or embody the things these symbols represent. People often confuse the outward display of symbols with the possession of the things those symbols represent.

> Wearing a cross is not the same as being a Christian, waving a flag is not the same as being free.

Despite claiming the copyright to many symbols of power, leaders of governments today have failed in the most serious regard. They have failed in their duty, their sacred duty, they're ONLY duty. They have failed to serve the sole function of their position, which is to foster a healthy society and to mediate a harmonic balance between civilization and the natural world. The ancient Egyptians called this condition Ma'at.

Ma'at was the sacred standard by which an ancient ruler's legitimacy could be judged.

If the ruler could not maintain the covenant between heaven and earth, in the form of health and prosperity for the people and the land, then their right to hold this sacred position could be revoked.

A ruler's failure to maintain the balance of Ma'at, would cause misfortunes to fall upon the people.

If a nation's ruler failed in their sacred duties, if they broke the essential laws of life, then the heavens would withhold rain, or bring it forth in floods. When the ruler had a diseased mind then diseases and plagues would visit the people.

When dangerous hordes threaten, when food becomes scarce, when society begins to fragment, when wealth has drained away in the cost of long wars—in short— when the kingdom is in turmoil—it's a sign.

> Turmoil is the mark of a kingdom whose ruler has lost the mandate of heaven.

To restore and maintain internal peace (Ma'at) there has always been the need for a sovereign power, one that can rise above warring factions and bring them into order. Long has humanity awaited the return of a powerful guiding light in the form of a leader who can provide civilization with a fixed point of reference, some sense of sanity amidst tragically chaotic waters.

The eventual and inevitable return of this light shares an archetypal theme with Christianity's belief in "the return of Christ."

Still one question remains to be answered: On judgment day, who will be held to account for "We the People's" abuses of power?

The Return of Legitimate Power

What would the return of legitimate power look like?

What object is capable of bearing the responsibility of sovereign rights? If not who, then what?

> Sovereignty is not only a transcendent principle, but also an object that embodies that principle.

What value shines so brightly that its existence represents the self-evident truth of a higher law?

What object is so great that only the highest God could have created it?

> The answer, of course, is the Sun. The return of legitimacy, is like the return of the Sun.

Who then can embody the sovereignty which is the gift of the Sun? Once, the answer to this question was simple and straightforward: only a king could embody the sovereign rights of the Sun.

However, once the King was ritually sacrificed, who remained to embody divine right? Who remained to reestablish Ma'at in the kingdom? Who, like the returning Sun, could resurrect the divine order on Earth?

This responsibility, it appears, has now fallen on the Sovereign Individual. For the sovereignty of the individual to exist, scattered rights must be consolidated and forged into an exercisable power.

> Rights only exist when a person holds them independently, in their own hands, and can exercise them.

Like gold, legitimacy must take a definite form to be real, it's too important a value to be ethereal. The word gold has no value in and of itself, neither does the idea of gold.

Only the substance of gold has value. Merely saying there's gold in the vault doesn't represent actual wealth. The same could be said of legitimate authority, we naively take it for granted there are securities to back the note.

Beyond the question of whether authority is backed by legitimate substance is the question "what makes total authority *theirs* by right?" For a thing of such immense importance and value, as total authority is, we can afford to make no assumptions.

What if we cower before a greenscreen of 'Authority?'

What if the 'elites' are not elite at all, but rather a group of sexually depraved, soulless junkies, hiding behind a Hollywood curtain pretending to be the Wizard of Oz?

The power to make laws, abrogate existing laws, amend obsolete laws, print money, declare wars, impose taxes and inflict punishments, must never fall into the wrong hands. This is the most important lesson from history.

So then, what are the wrong hands?

The concept of sovereignty applies to all matters important for establishing and maintaining domestic peace. When the validity of a law is no longer based in divine will, it proceeds merely from self-interest, business opportunism and political cunning.

Detached from divine will, government has become a concept describing the complete possession, or ownership, of governing authority by a certain group, unbound by the law of God, moral law or natural law.

Without legitimacy, implementing compliance through coercion and psychological warfare has steadily become the agreed-upon policy, as governments have now waged a multigenerational war against the conscious awakening of the population with the hopes of gaining full technological dominance before this awakening occurs.

Throughout history, humanity has consistently been plagued with the question: "Who gets to decide the fate of the world? Who or what can be considered legitimate authority?"

> Democracies suggest that "we the people" hold this power.

As representatives of "we the people," can we as sovereign individuals, choose instead to invest this power directly in ourselves? Or do we still believe that it is necessary to contract our right of self-determination out to others?

If so, should this contract go to those superiorly trained and more competent, like was the case with ancient Kings and Queens, or should the contract go to those far less competent but far more numerous, as is the case with popular democracy. Is there any alternative to surrendering one's political fate to the opinion of the manipulated masses?

From the pharaohs of ancient Egypt, to the monarchs of Europe, to the emperors of China, to the most recent American elections, the question of who holds the power has been a contentious one.

Does the authority to govern come from above, as in "divine law" or does it come from below as in "mob rule?" Or perhaps, from within?

This shift from divine rule to secular rule has brought forth important questions. Some of the most obvious are:

What special touch transforms revolutionary outlaws into lawgiving founding fathers?

What authority grants a claim of ownership on a non-consenting population?

Whose signature is required to authorize a monopoly on violence?

Who owns the trademark to authority?

The transition from "rule from above," in the form of sovereign rule according to divine law, to "rule from below," in the form of democracies held in place through mass psychological manipulation and economic coercion, is a complex one.

Throughout history, we have seen the rise and fall of various forms of government, each with its own unique set of challenges. From the Roman Republic to the French Revolution, the question of legitimate authority has been a constant theme.

The French Revolution, supposedly inspired by the democratic ideas of the age of reason, became a bloody movement of mob violence which ultimately gave rise to a totalitarian emperor. When commenting on his rise to power, Napoleon simply stated that he found the French crown in the gutter, reached down and picked it up.

These historical events illustrate the ever-evolving nature of legitimate authority and the struggles that have arisen in the quest for it. The question remains, who holds the rights to ultimate power over the individual and what copyright constitutes legitimate authority?

Currently, this authority to rule is bought and sold at political auction every four years. Like slaves at the market, the question of every election is whom will "the people" be sold to next?

> Sovereignty is the backbone of human rights, it is the foundation upon which all rights are built.

It is the source of power that ensures the inalienable rights given to us by our creator are protected and upheld. Without sovereignty, these rights would be nothing more than empty promises.

Corporate sovereignty has only served to strip the individual of their power and make them nothing more than a corporate share.

Such is the case now, with the rise of supra-national entities, fictitious phantoms operating solely in their own interest and loyal to no individual and no nation. These are shadow organizations whose crimes can be committed without repercussion because blame can merely be placed on a faceless entity hidden behind a web of justifications disguised as democratic considerations.

It is time to shift the focus from these fictitious entities to the individual. Each and every one of us has the right to invoke the sovereign power of self-determination. A Sovereign Nation is a nation which truly serves the greater good of the individual. It is time to shift the focus back to the individual and the protection of their sovereign rights.

The Wrong Hands

In a popular democracy, the illusion of freedom is perpetuated through the facade of "popular" sovereignty in which ultimate decision making authority is outwardly vested in the winning contestant of a popularity contest.

The masses are given a mere pebble with which to vote. They are led to believe that they have a say in the shaping of their political system, that their pebble holds weight in the grand scheme of things. But the truth is, democracy is nothing more than a game of numbers.

The pile of pebbles that holds the most weight, no matter how questionable or misshapen, is enthroned as authority. But how many pebbles does it take to shift the balance of metric tons of fraud and deception?

In this system, the power lies not with the people, but with whoever or whatever tallies the pebbles. Even the value of this pebble, the currency of democracy, is inflated through counterfeiting, leaving many to question its actual value.

The price of this system includes the involuntary surrender of the individual's natural rights to a collective raising of hands. If depression, mental illness, drug addiction, and media manipulation become common influences in a democratic society, how could this not affect the integrity of the vote?

What happens if a generation of heavily medicated, bipolar, manic depressive, obsessive compulsive doom scrollers with ADHD become the deciding vote in decisions of leadership and state? Where would democracy's halo be then?

If democracy wants to maintain its claim of being the only patented process for legitimizing authority, then maintaining a high degree of intelligence and sanity in its population must be considered its first priority. Democracy is like a mirror, reflecting either the beauty or degeneracy of a population back onto itself.

Democracy works best within the confines of relatively small populations of highly intelligent people, who possess a somewhat homogeneous character, a shared system of beliefs and a congenial disposition toward each other.

In the circus of popular democracy, the illusion of power is given to the masses through the symbolic act of voting. But in reality, the true power lies in the hands of an anonymous few. The individual's voice is drowned out by the sheer volume of pebbles cast, and their vote becomes nothing more than a drop in a leaky bucket.

The true decision-making power is left in the hands of those who hold the purse strings and who manipulate both voters and the vote.

Democracy, in this sense, is nothing more than a facade, a theatrical performance to pacify the masses while true power remains in the hands of allocators of capital. The individual is left with little to no agency in shaping their own future, and their participation in the democratic process is reduced to a mere formality.

> In the words of Fredrick Nietzsche, "Independence of soul – that is the question at issue!"

There are many today who claim to value freedom, yet willingly sacrifice it upon the altar of political correctness, constraining others through social obligation to bend a knee to ever more radical agendas. Many condemn slavery yet submit to, and even invite it, in new and evermore pernicious forms.

Individual freedom, as a value, is above the concern of social consensus. True freedom, as the founding fathers knew, requires sacrifices, including the sacrifice of ideas and institutions that seek to undermine it.

Contemporary governments make claims and demands on our rights, our resources, our attention and our allegiance, all in the name of unknown abbreviated agencies marauding behind the mask of "the state."

We often think of these claims on our life as a fee for services, but they are not. They are an obligation to support the state. It's not an exchange, it is a contract, *a claim on our lives.*

The terrible threat of this monster emerges, not in the authority of the state's basic laws but in its capacity to make a total claim upon not only a territory and its wealth, but even on the lives of those existing within said territory. This claim now extends well beyond almost every reasonable boundary or legitimate justification.

Some governments are prepared to threaten world destruction as a condition of their own existence. They believe that the continuation of their particular form of government, whether democratic, communistic, socialist or dictatorial, is beyond all importance, even beyond the importance of life itself.

Some worship false gods, some worship false governments. They are essentially the same, both demand a total claim on our lives, and both are willing to destroy the world to maintain their position.

The preservation of one's own life is an inalienable right, a fundamental principle of nature. It is the very essence of our existence. To sacrifice that right, to willingly surrender it to an illegitimate authority, is a violation of the natural order, a transgression of basic human dignity. It is a tragedy of the highest order for civilization to be led to destruction by the actions of those who have no legitimate claim or competence to govern.

From the perspective of contemporary governments, its citizens are its property, not its people. The state is in the same position as the slave owner.

Like the king in chess, who cannot voluntarily put itself into check, a person can not legally contract away their sovereignty.

Many people are now rejecting the presupposition that institutions have the right to make an absolute claim on their lives. It has been said that, when states fail, it's because their God has died. They no longer believe that the institutions and government express the sovereign voice. Such is the case now. Across the globe, the feeling of estrangement from contemporary forms of government is becoming ever more universal.

Sovereignty is the ultimate value, the one that must be upheld at all costs. It is the foundation of our autonomy, the source of our transcendence.

It is through sacrifice of falsehoods that sovereignty can be preserved. In so doing, we lay the foundation for a great sovereign nation, one that is built on the relentless pursuit of autonomy, of self-governance, and of self-determination.

This is the essence of true freedom, the ultimate goal of all sacrifices. Let us not relinquish this value, for anything or anyone.

> It is our duty to uphold it, to defend it, and to preserve it for future generations.

CHAPTER FIVE

The Sovereign Nation

A New Dawn

A Sovereign Nation is a country that is governed by the principle of self-rule, where the people possess their own independent power and authority.

At the most fundamental level, our physical body is made up of cells, just as a nation is made up of individuals. In the body, many problems can be traced back to interactions occurring at the cellular level. In societies, many problems begin and end with the individual. Like the atom in physics, or the hexagon in a colony of bees, the individual is the fundamental unit from which the whole of society is composed.

It's this individual unit, that actually represents the core identity of "We the People." Yet current political efforts attempt to deny and diminish the individual's independent authority while simultaneously overwhelming them with demands and obligations allegedly placed on it *by authority* of "We the People."

One of the key concepts of a Sovereign Nation is the idea of a Sovereign Individual. This is a person who recognizes their own sovereignty and responsibly exercises their own power and autonomy, rather than being constantly subject to the questionable will of others.

The benefits of a Sovereign Nation are many. One of the most important is that it allows for greater freedom and autonomy for its citizens. In a Sovereign Nation, people bear a greater weight of responsibility than in a welfare state. When it comes to individual decisions that affect only them, they are the final decision making authority. Obviously, this requires the maintenance of an educated, responsible and psychologically healthy population.

The Sovereign Nation, as a reflection of the Sovereign Individual, must be able to protect its own interests and defend its sovereignty, rather than be subject to control by outside powers.

Many benefits would be obtained by such a Sovereign Nation. A Sovereign Nation allows for a greater sense of community and shared identity among its citizens. When people are taught to self-govern to a greater degree, they are more likely to feel a sense of ownership and responsibility for their country.

This would lead to greater civic engagement and participation in the political process, as well as a more vibrant and dynamic society.

12 Laws of the Sovereign Nation

The sovereign individual is the ultimate benefactor of the authority and power of the government. The individual is the ultimate unit of society.

> The sovereign individual has the right to govern themselves and make their own decisions.
>
> The individual's sovereignty and rights are protected by the Sovereign Nation.
>
> The government's role is to protect the individual's natural rights and property.
>
> The individual has the right to freely express themselves without fear of censorship or repression.
>
> The government is limited in its power and authority by the rights of the individual.
>
> The individual has the right to participate in the political process and hold elected officials accountable.
>
> The individual has the right to a fair trial and due process of law.

The government does not have the right to infringe upon the individual's religious or personal beliefs.

The government is accountable to the people and can be changed or abolished if it fails to protect their rights.

The individual has the right to own property and to use it as they see fit.

The Individual's divine right cannot be taken away by the government. Like life, Divine Right, is the gift of the Sun.

CHAPTER SIX

A Guide to Writing

Your Own Declaration of Independence and Constitution

Writing your own declaration of independence as a creative practice is an exercise in self-discovery and self-expression that allows you to define your values, goals, and aspirations.

Part 1: The Importance of Sovereignty

Sovereignty is the supreme authority within a political entity, such as a nation-state. It is the power to govern and make decisions without external interference or influence.

Self-determination and self-sovereignty are closely related concepts that refer to a people's or group's ability to govern themselves and make decisions about their own affairs.

Without the ability to govern and make decisions for ourselves, we lose our freedom and autonomy. A loss of sovereignty can lead to a loss of control over our own lives and the direction of our society. It can also lead to oppression and injustice, as decisions are made by outside forces with little regard for the well-being of the people affected by them.

One way of understanding the concept of sovereignty is through the lens of natural law. Natural law is a philosophical and legal theory that holds that certain rights and responsibilities are inherent to human nature and exist independently of any government or institution.

According to this theory, the human soul is inherently noble and dignified, and sovereignty is necessary to protect and uphold this inherent nobility and dignity.

Part 2: The Declaration of Independence as a Template

The Declaration of Independence is a document that was adopted by the Continental Congress on July 4, 1776. It announced that the thirteen American colonies, then at war with Great Britain, were no longer subject to British rule and were now independent states. The Declaration of Independence was written primarily by Thomas Jefferson and is considered one of the most important documents in American history.

The Declaration of Independence is significant for several reasons. Firstly, it was a statement of the colonies' right to self-government and self-determination.

Secondly, it set forth the principles of liberty and democracy that have become the cornerstone of American politics and society.

Thirdly, it served as a powerful symbol of the American Revolution, inspiring other colonies to join the fight for independence.

The Declaration of Independence can serve as a template for writing your own declaration of independence. The document is divided into three main parts: the preamble, the bill of rights, and the grievances.

The preamble is an introduction that sets forth the purpose of the document and the principles upon which it is based. The bill of rights is a list of rights and freedoms that the people are entitled to. The grievances are a list of complaints against the previous government and its actions.

The preamble of the Declaration of Independence begins with the famous words "When in the Course of human events, it becomes necessary for one people to dissolve the political bands which have connected them with another, and to assume among the powers of the earth, the separate and equal station to which the Laws of Nature and of Nature's God entitle them." This sets the tone and purpose of the document, which is to break away from the rule of another power and establish a separate and equal station.

The bill of rights of the Declaration of Independence includes phrases such as "life, liberty, and the pursuit of happiness" and "all men are created equal" which are considered the foundation of the American political system and society, and still inspire people all over the world.

The grievances in the Declaration of Independence are a list of complaints against the British king, such as "He has refused his Assent to Laws, the most wholesome and necessary for the public good." These grievances were considered justification for the colonies to break away from British rule.

The Declaration of Independence is a significant document in American history that served as a statement of the colonies' right to self-government and self-determination, set forth the principles of liberty and democracy and served as a powerful symbol of the American Revolution.

Part 3: Writing Your Own Declaration of Independence

The Declaration of Independence is a powerful and enduring document that has stood the test of time. It is a powerful reminder of the importance of self-government and self-determination, and serves as a powerful symbol of the principles of liberty and democracy. In this chapter, we will guide you on how to write your own declaration of independence, and how to use it as a tool for self-discovery and self-empowerment.

Step 1: *Identify your Values, Goals, and Aspirations*

The first step in writing your own declaration of independence is to identify your core values, goals, and aspirations. These are the things that are most important to you and that you are willing to fight for. Some prompts to help you identify your values, goals, and aspirations include:

What are the most important things in your life?

What are your long-term goals and aspirations?

Step 2: *Write a Preamble*

The preamble of your declaration of independence should set forth the purpose of the document and the principles upon which it is based. Some prompts to help you write your preamble include:

> What is the purpose of your declaration of independence?

> What are the principles that you believe are essential to your well-being and happiness?

Step 3: *Write a Bill of Rights*

The bill of rights of your declaration of independence should be a list of rights and freedoms that you believe are essential to your well-being and happiness. Some prompts to help you write your bill of rights include:

> What are the rights and freedoms that you believe are essential to your well-being and happiness?

> What are the things that you would be willing to fight for?

Step 4: *Write a List of Grievances*

The grievances of your declaration of independence should be a list of complaints against any force that is preventing you from achieving your values, goals, and aspirations. Some prompts to help you write your list of grievances include:

> What are the things that are preventing you from achieving your values, goals, and aspirations?

> What are the things that you believe are unjust or oppressive?

> What are the things that you would like to change?

Step 5: *Finalize your Declaration*

Once you have completed the preamble, bill of rights, and list of grievances, it is time to finalize your declaration of independence. Review your document and make any necessary revisions. Once you are satisfied with your document, you can sign and date it.

Your declaration of independence is a powerful and personal document that reflects your values, goals, and aspirations. It is a powerful reminder of the importance of self-government and self-determination, and serves as a powerful symbol of the principles of liberty and democracy. Use it as a tool for self-discovery and self-empowerment, and as a reminder of the things that you believe are worth fighting for.

Writing your own declaration of independence is a powerful and empowering process that can help you identify your values, goals, and aspirations, and serve as a tool for self-discovery and self-empowerment. By following the step-by-step guide provided in this chapter, you can write a powerful and persuasive document that reflects your unique perspective on the world and the things that you believe are worth fighting for.

Writing your own Sovereign Constitution

Writing one's own "constitution" as a self-development practice can provide a number of benefits for the sovereign individual. From a psychological perspective, creating a personal constitution allows for self-reflection and self-awareness, helping individuals to understand their values, principles, and goals. This understanding can lead to greater personal agency, autonomy, and self-direction, which are key components of self-actualization psychology.

From a mythological perspective, the act of creating a personal constitution can also be seen as a way of claiming one's freedom. This can be a powerful symbolic act that affirms the individual's autonomy and agency, and can serve as a reminder to live in accordance with one's values and principles.

From a legal perspective, a personal constitution serves as a binding document that holds the individual accountable to their values, principles, and goals. It provides a clear framework for decision-making and behavior, and can help to ensure consistency and integrity in personal actions.

Overall, writing a personal constitution can serve as a powerful tool for personal growth and self-actualization. It allows individuals to reflect on their values and principles, set specific and meaningful goals, and take action to live in accordance with those values and goals. In this way, it can help the sovereign individual to achieve their full potential and live a more fulfilling life.

Components of writing your own Constitution

Purpose: Clearly state the purpose of the constitution, such as to guide personal behavior, set goals, and establish values.

Values: Identify and list personal values that align with the purpose of the constitution. These values will serve as the foundation for decision-making and goal setting.

Principles: Establish a set of principles that align with the values and purpose of the constitution. These principles will guide behavior and decision-making.

Goals: Set specific, measurable, and attainable goals that align with the values and principles of the constitution. These goals will serve as the road map for personal development and self-actualization.

Accountability: Establish a system for accountability, such as regular check-ins and progress reports, to ensure adherence to the values, principles, and goals outlined in the constitution.

Flexibility: Allow for flexibility and adaptability in the constitution, recognizing that personal values, principles, and goals may change over time.

Review and Revise: Regularly review and revise the constitution as needed to ensure that it continues to align with personal values, principles, and goals.

Action: Make a commitment to take action in line with the values, principles, and goals outlined in the constitution.

Justification for the Sovereign Manifesto

In the Sovereign Manifesto, we have outlined the importance of the Sovereign Individual and Sovereign Nation in achieving a holistic, healthy order in today's society. Our justifications for this manifesto are rooted in the life force of the sun, the inherent nobility and dignity of the human soul, and the principles of natural law.

> The sun, the source of all life on earth, also symbolizes the life force within each and every one of us.

Just as the sun shines down upon the earth, providing light and warmth, so too does the life force within each of us shine out to the world from us, when we are at our best.

When we are at our most brilliant, our words and deeds carry the signature of the sovereign sun. It is by the light of the sun that we, like all life on earth, receive the power to live, to grow, and to achieve our full potential. This life force, this inner sun, is the source of our power, the shining light of our divine right.

The inherent nobility and dignity of the human soul is a foundational element of our justifications. Each individual is born with the inherent right to self-determination and self-sovereignty, which is reflected in the principles of natural law. This means that no external force or authority has the power to infringe upon the rights of the individual, as outlined in our constitution.

Furthermore, the Sovereign Individual and Sovereign Nation must abide by the principle of non-aggression, meaning that they should not initiate unjustified and unwarranted force against others. They must also respect the rights of others and work towards the common good. These principles are rooted in natural law and are necessary for the protection of individual rights, freedom and the overall well-being of society.

In summary, the justifications for the Sovereign Manifesto are rooted in natural law, the ultimate expression of which is the life force of the sun, the same sun, which is the source of the individual's own consciousness.

CHAPTER SEVEN

The Sovereign Sun

The sun, a symbol of enlightenment and redemption, has been revered throughout history as a powerful political and spiritual symbol of sovereignty. For both the individual and nation, the sun represents the embodiment of nobility, dignity, strength, and joy. In the cycles of human civilization, the sun has been a beacon of hope, illuminating the darkness and leading us towards redemption.

For the individual, the sun represents the sovereign self that is free by divine right. The sun is the watchful eye of the most high, illuminating the path towards self-discovery and self-actualization. It is the source of energy and vitality, the giver of life and light. By aligning ourselves with the energy of the sun, we tap into our own source of power.

> Symbolically, the sun represents
> strength and unity.

The sun is the symbol of the Sovereign Nation's identity, the source of its power and vitality. A nation that aligns itself with the energy of the sun, becomes a beacon of hope and progress for the world, a shining example of what humanity can achieve when united under a common purpose.

In many mythologies, the sun is seen as a symbol of redemption, the light that guides us towards a better future. The ancient Egyptians, Incas, Mayans, and Indo-Europeans all revered the sun as the giver of life and the ruler of the heavens. They built temples and pyramids to reflect the divine will of heaven, and through their spiritual alignment with the sun, were able to create a continuity of empires that lasted for millennia.

The sun is also a symbol of the cyclical nature of human civilization, the reminder that there is always hope for redemption and rebirth. Just as the sun rises and sets every day, human civilization also goes through cycles of growth and decline. Just as the sun always rises again, so too can human civilization be reborn and renewed.

The sun is a powerful political and spiritual symbol of sovereignty, for both the individual and the nation, illuminating the path towards redemption and uniting humanity under a common purpose.

Universal Solar Spirituality: A Sustainable Solution

The world is in need of a spiritual reorientation, a reconnection with universal energies that has been lost in the modern age. It is a spiritual bond between the individual and the sun, between the microcosm and the macrocosm, that is the key to regenerating the world and restoring balance to human consciousness.

Throughout history, great civilizations have thrived under the guidance of solar oriented forms of spirituality, and it is time for us to rediscover this ancient wisdom and apply it to the contemporary age. It is this sun-centered spiritual orientation which has the power to simultaneously redeem and resolve the conflict between spirituality and science.

The sun, as the most dominant influence of our solar system, represents the source of all life and energy.

> The sun is the embodiment of the Universal Solar Spirit, the force that brings life and vitality to the world.

Ancient civilizations such as the Egyptians, the Incas, and the Mayans, and the Indo-Europeans understood the importance of the sun in their spiritual beliefs. This spiritual alignment led to a continuity of empires that spanned almost uninterrupted for millennia. It is largely due to the fact that its spiritual alignment has been lost, that humanity now finds itself in a panic-stricken web of social and environmental problems too immense for contemporary political and spiritual models to fix.

There is no more time for spot treating the problems of the world. Solutions must be all encompassing. *The Sovereign Manifesto* offers a diagnosis, remedy and prescription for this spiritual sickness.

This spiritual bond between the individual and the sun brings with it a sense of unity and purpose, one that could help humanity to clarify its role, not only as stewards of the Earth, but as stewards of the solar system.

Furthermore, this spiritual connection with the sun can also have a profound impact on the environment. By understanding our role as stewards of the solar system, we will be more inclined to preserve and protect the earth and its resources. We will also be more aware of our impact on the natural world and make conscious choices in determining right action.

Here are just a few ways the sun represents a valuable spiritual ethic:

> As a source of light, warmth and life, representing the power of the sun to sustain and nourish the earth.

Through its associations with power, energy, and vitality, representing the sun's power to drive the cycles of life and growth.

Through its association with creation, renewal, and regeneration, which represents the sun's role in the cycles of the seasons and the cycles of life and death.

Through its association with wisdom, insight, and understanding, which represents the sun's ability to reveal and illuminate the world.

Through its association with guidance and direction, representing the sun's role in providing a point of orientation for navigation.

Being associated with strength, endurance and protection, representing the sun's ability to protect and defend its followers.

Five benefits a Universal Solar Religion would bring to the World:

1. Increased unity and harmony

A universal Solar religion could bring people of different cultures, ethnicities, and backgrounds together, promoting unity and harmony among people. It could provide a shared belief system and values that could help to reduce conflicts and misunderstandings.

2. Greater focus on environmental stewardship

A universal Solar religion that emphasizes the importance of the sun and the natural world could inspire people to take better care of the environment. By recognizing the sun as the source of all life and energy, people would be more likely to respect and care for the environment.

3. Greater sense of purpose and meaning

A universal Solar religion could provide people with a greater sense of purpose and meaning. By connecting to the divine will of the sun and aligning with it, people would be more likely to reach their full potential and make positive contributions to the world.

4. Increased spiritual connection

A universal Solar religion could provide people with a deeper sense of spiritual connection, helping them to feel more connected to the world around them. The sun could become a powerful symbol of hope and transcendence, providing a sense of something greater than themselves.

5. Increased awareness and understanding

A universal Solar religion could increase awareness and understanding of different cultures, history and belief systems. It could foster mutual respect and understanding among people.

True Will is the understanding of one's own unique purpose and path in life.

CHAPTER EIGHT

Sovereign Ethics

The creation of a sovereign nation of sovereign individuals requires a specific set of ethics, rooted in the concepts of sovereignty, true will, divine right, and self-actualization. These ethics form the foundation upon which such a society must be built, for without them, the nation would be nothing more than a hollow shell, lacking the vital principles that give it meaning and purpose.

Sovereignty, in its most basic form, is the recognition and acceptance of one's own authority and autonomy. It is the understanding that each individual is the ultimate authority in their own lives and has the right to be primarily governed by their own inner guidance. This principle is essential for a nation of sovereign individuals, for without it, individuals would be subject to the will of others, rather than their own.

True Will is the understanding of one's own unique purpose and path in life. It is the recognition that each individual is here to fulfill a specific role and that it is their duty to discover and align with this role. In a nation of sovereign individuals, it is essential that each individual is encouraged and empowered to discover and fulfill their True Will, for without it, the nation would lack the authenticity and richness that comes from the unique contributions of its citizens.

Divine Right is the understanding that each individual has a sacred responsibility to govern themselves according to their own conscience and inner guidance. It is the recognition that each individual has a unique connection to the divine and that it is their duty to honor and follow this connection. In a nation of sovereign individuals, it is essential that individuals are free to govern themselves according to their own inner guidance, for without this freedom, the nation would lack the spiritual depth and richness that comes from honoring the divine within each individual.

Self-actualization is the process of becoming the best version of oneself.

It is the understanding that each individual has the potential to become their most authentic and fulfilled self and that it is their duty to work towards this goal. In a nation of sovereign individuals, it is essential that individuals are encouraged and supported in their journey of self-actualization, for without this encouragement, the nation would lack the vitality and richness that comes from the growth and development of its citizens.

In the words of the philosopher Aristotle, "Ethics is not just about the individual, but about the collective as well." A just society is one in which each individual can fulfill their potential and contribute to the common good.

The ethics of sovereignty, true will, divine right, and self-actualization are essential for creating a sovereign nation of sovereign individuals, for they provide the foundation upon which such a society can flourish. It is the duty of each individual to uphold these ethics, to govern themselves according to their own conscience and inner guidance, and to work towards the betterment of the collective.

Ethics provide the foundation upon which such a society can flourish, and it is the duty of each individual to uphold them, to govern themselves accordingly. It is only through the cultivation of these ethics that a nation of sovereign individuals can truly come to fruition and be a shining example of a just and harmonious society.

Sovereign Values

Sovereignty is the supreme authority within a political entity, such as a nation or state. It is the power to govern oneself, free from external interference or control. The values of the Sovereign Individual are closely tied to this concept, as they embody the belief in self-governance and self-determination.

The value of sovereignty cannot be overstated, as it is the foundation of a free society. Without sovereignty, individuals would be at the mercy of external forces, unable to make decisions for themselves and shape their own destiny. Sovereignty allows for the protection of individual rights and freedoms, as well as the ability to hold leaders accountable for their actions.

> The Sovereign Individual values self-reliance, independence, and personal responsibility.

These values are essential for a healthy society, as they promote individual initiative and creativity, and foster a sense of community and mutual respect. The Sovereign Individual understands that their success is the result of their own actions and efforts, and they take pride in their accomplishments.

However, sovereignty also requires the acceptance of responsibility for one's actions and the consequences that come with them. The Sovereign Individual accepts that their freedom comes with the responsibility to respect the freedom of others, and understand that their actions have an impact on their community and society as a whole.

In today's globalized world, the concept of sovereignty and the values of the Sovereign Individual are more important than ever. The ability to govern oneself and shape one's own destiny is essential for a free and prosperous society. It is the responsibility of each and every one of us to uphold the values of sovereignty and the Sovereign Individual, in order to ensure a bright future for ourselves and future generations.

Ma'at: The Spirit of Legitimacy

Ma'at is a concept central to ancient Egyptian religion and society, and it represents the balance and harmony of the universe. The goddess Ma'at personifies this concept and is often depicted as a woman with an ostrich feather in her hair.

The ostrich feather was chosen as a symbol for Ma'at because it was believed to be a symbol of truth and justice. In ancient Egypt, the ostrich was considered a powerful and regal bird, and its feathers were highly prized for their beauty and symbolic value.

According to Egyptian mythology, during the judgment of the dead, the heart of the deceased was weighed against the feather of Ma'at. If the heart was found to be free of sin and lighter than the feather, the deceased was considered to have lived a just life and would be granted entry into the afterlife. However, if the heart was found to be heavy with sin, it would be devoured by a monster, and the deceased would be denied entry into the afterlife.

The image of Ma'at with an ostrich feather in her hair is a representation of her role in the judgment of the dead and her power to maintain truth and justice in the universe. The feather symbolizes the importance of living a just life and following the principles of Ma'at in order to achieve a favorable judgment in the afterlife.

> The pharaohs were considered
> the embodiment of Ma'at and were
> responsible for maintaining it in society.

Ma'at was considered the foundation of the natural order and was seen as the source of all life and creation. The pharaohs were believed to have been chosen by the gods to maintain Ma'at, and their rule was seen as a reflection of the divine order. They were responsible for ensuring the stability of society by promoting justice, truth, and balance.

In practical terms, this meant that the pharaohs were responsible for ensuring that the laws were fair, that the economy was stable, and that the land was fertile. They also had to ensure that the temples and shrines were maintained, and that the connection to either God or Gods was honored.

Politically, adherence to Ma'at was a duty required of all pharaohs. The pharaohs were seen as the representatives of the gods on earth, and their rule was seen as a reflection of the divine order. This concept beautifully illustrated the balance of the pharaohs' authority. In this model, great power was tempered by equally great restraint, represented by the crook and flail.

The crook, also known as the heka, was a symbol of the pharaoh's power and authority. It was a long, curved staff with a hook at one end, similar to a shepherd's crook. The crook symbolized the pharaoh's ability to guide and lead his people, much like a shepherd guiding his flock. It also represented the pharaoh's ability to maintain order and justice in his kingdom.

The flail, also known as the nekhakha, was a symbol of the pharaoh's restraint and responsibility. It was a whip-like instrument with three or more beads or balls at the end, and it was used to separate the wheat from the chaff during the harvesting process. The flail symbolized the pharaoh's responsibility to ensure that his people were provided for and that the land was productive. It also represented the pharaoh's ability to punish wrongdoers and maintain order through force, if necessary.

Together, the crook and flail symbolized the pharaoh's dual role as both a powerful ruler and a responsible leader. They represented the balance between power and restraint that was necessary for a successful and just reign. The pharaoh's ability to wield the crook and flail was seen as a manifestation of his divine power and authority, and their use during ceremonies and rituals emphasized the pharaoh's role as the link between the gods and the people.

CHAPTER NINE

Sovereign Consciousness

Sovereign Consciousness is a state of being in which an individual has a deep understanding and connection to their inner self, and is able to make decisions and take actions that align with their true values and desires. This state of being is characterized by self-awareness, self-acceptance, and self-responsibility.

The rising of a Sovereign Nation is akin to the dawn of a new Sun.

Just as the Sun's light brings new life and vitality to the Earth, so too will the light of sovereignty bring new life and vitality to humanity. The spirit of this manifesto is about regenerating the vitality of civilization.

> As the Sun rises, it dispels the darkness.

In the same way, the light of sovereignty dispels the darkness of oppression, manipulation, and control, and brings with it a renewal of energy, and a complete structural reorientation for civilization.

This is not just a change of governance, but a change of paradigms, a new era for humanity. We have the power to create a world where each individual is free to live as master in their own relative domain, according to their own conscience as guided by the ancient principle of Ma'at.

In what other way could the collective will of the people become, in time, truly Sovereign?

Transcendentalism and spiritual sovereignty

Ralph Waldo Emerson (1803-1882) and a small group composed mainly of Unitarian ministers formed the Transcendental Club. Transcendentalism is a philosophy that emphasizes the soul's inborn knowledge of ultimate realities of the universe, and emphasizes the soul's transcendence in life as the fundamental goal of man.

In Transcendentalism, each soul is seen as carrying the whole of the cosmos within it, interconnected yet independent in power and truth. Emerson declared, "That is always best which gives me to myself. The sublime is excited in me by the great stoical doctrine, Obey thyself. That which shows God in me, fortifies me. That which shows God out of me, makes me a wart and a wen."

Emerson suggests, like Odin, that we give ourselves to ourselves; that each of us can become a cosmos rather than a chaos.

Each soul is the maker of its own ethical self, yet connected in the sense that truth discovered within the deepest part of the soul touches on truth that transcends apparent differences. Truth, being self evident, is connected to the ultimate realities of the universe and, therefore, is the same for all men. Emerson believed in the soul's inborn knowledge of ultimate realities.

"We are now men, and must accept in the highest mind the same transcendent destiny; and not pinched in a corner, not cowards fleeing before a revolution, but redeemers, and benefactors, pious aspirants to be noble clay under the Almighty effort, let us advance on Chaos and the Dark."

Emerson insists that humankind is the redeemer; the essence of virtue and truth is within the soul, and the individual is able to press forward against Chaos and Darkness, attaining transcendence and harmony.

Obedience to one's own soul is the path to salvation: "To believe your own thought, to believe that what is true for you in your private heart, is true for all men - that is genius," declared Emerson.

In "The American Scholar," Emerson asserted, "It is one soul which animates all men." It is this same "Sol," the ancient name of the Sun, which animates all of life in the solar system.

Transcendentalists affirm that humanity has the capacity to find illumination and salvation independent of church dogma. The individual rises in self-trust: "In self-trust, all virtues are comprehended." Self-trust leads to harmony of the individual soul with God.

Transcendentalism celebrates the interconnectedness of souls that happens simultaneously as each person finds their own role and path in life.

Autonomy ought to be our aim, though Emerson intends a healing of the self, rather than alienation from society. Humankind has the ability to face the chaos and darkness in society and the world; each soul can break through the disharmony and find meaning within itself as well as within the cosmos.

Mankind, a Microcosm born from the Macrocosm

Transcendental values of the self-empowering soul resonate with the search for meaning wrestled with in Faust by Johann Wolfgang von Goethe [1749-1832].

In "The American Scholar," Emerson wrote that Goethe, "The most modern of the moderns, has shown us, as none ever did, the genius of the ancients."

From the Prologue of Faust, Goethe introduced the idea of individualistic society's sense of autonomy and disharmony in the universe. Archangel Raphael says, "The sun intones, in ancient tourney [ancient song],/ With brother spheres, a rival air" Goethe was referring to the "harmony of the spheres," a Pythagorean teaching in which each sphere in the solar system emits a tone that harmonizes with the tones of all the other spheres.

Pythagorean mysticism asserted an ordered cosmos (the word cosmos originally meant "order"), wherein everything exists as a harmonious whole in concordance with the symmetries and correlations intrinsic to the numbers and their geometrical representations: This was called Harmonices Mundi, or Harmony of the world.

The microcosm represents the individual and the macrocosm the universe. In Nature, Emerson emphasized the striving of the individual soul as central along the path to transcendence and unity with the cosmos.

Emerson asserted, "A man is a god in ruins….the dwarf of himself."

The potential in humanity to struggle in its search for meaning will result in a transcendence of the immanent, yet the struggle toward harmony within oneself and the cosmos is an arduous one, a difficult striving of opposing forces.

Emerson stressed that the "reason why the world lacks unity, and lies broken and in heaps, is, because man is disunited with himself. He cannot be a naturalist, until he satisfies all the demands of the spirit."

As with Goethe, Emerson understood the disharmony and striving within the soul and without in the cosmos. Each soul, though dwarfed and in ruins, must be accountable in the personal path of seeking integration and meaning in order to be illumined in spirit and find harmony through transcendence.

Furthermore, humanity's condition as a god in ruins has caused it to become a follower of false governments, false idols, and distorted god-concepts.

Demotion to the role of mere follower displaces the cosmic power within the human being, exacerbating inner disunity.

The creative and cosmic power within man, to Emerson, is evident, yet dormant. The self-healing capacity of the human spirit, and the capability of "restoring to the world original and eternal beauty, is solved by the redemption of the soul."

The possibility of cosmic restoration lies with the human soul. Emerson put responsibility upon the individual to "build, therefore your own world." He had every faith that the good in humanity could conquer all disunity, all evil.

As we have seen, Goethe's disharmony in the universe serves as a platform for Faust's struggles through the process of self-transformation. Goethe presents a universe of disharmony. Yet, even without harmony on the macrocosmic level, the individual (the microcosm) may strive and eventually achieve its own inner harmony.

The connection between the soul and the cosmos encompasses science and spirit; the head and heart are in a relationship with terra firma and the solar system.

Similar to Emerson's claim that the search for meaning is through the striving of the soul, Goethe's Faust takes a path of self-realization within a cosmology that asserts a God who supports an individualistic journey to enlightenment.

Faust has set himself upon a sort of transcendentalist path of finding his true self. He has gone beyond the "holy sacraments" of the church to engage the cosmos itself and find his true self in relation to it. In fact, for transcendentalists and Faust, nothing is static, all is in flux, all is in a state of becoming, and each must strive on his own to discover harmony and the true self.

Goethe revealed Faust's journey to self-realization as a complex path, involving the synthesizing of the disharmonic duplicity within his own soul, a synthesis that will bring him into harmony with God.

Self-realization comes only when the person has wrestled with the dark and light sides within oneself. For Faust, striving toward knowledge of the self is the path to harmony and transcendence of the self. God, who for Faust pervades everything, is the elusive invisible hand that can be sensed and felt, and leads the person who is striving toward self-realization.

Every individual or microcosm, is an intimate part of the macrocosm. All that exists is pervaded by God; and all are in a state of becoming. Goethe's God reaches beyond the traditional Western Christian definition.

Faust breaks many rules when he turns from following the sacramental life of the church. Faust is, in many ways, Emerson's ideal transcendentalist: He chose to become his own sage, strove down a path toward self-realization, finding ultimate union within himself, with the cosmos, and with God.

In "Self-Reliance," Emerson declared that each soul should become his or her own sage, independently striving toward self-realization. He bemoaned, "Man is apologetic. He is no longer upright. He dares not say 'I think,' 'I am,' but quotes some saint or sage. ... He cannot be happy and strong until he too lives with nature in the present, above time."

Faust's struggle involves engaging light and dark forces. All souls have the potential to harmonize the light side and shadow side of their own microcosm in the present.

Emerson realized that the journey to unity and harmony is one of change and inconsistency, of trial and error. In a universe of contention, conflict and uncertainty, the striving soul will shift in its expression: "A foolish consistency is the hobgoblin of little minds."

Emerson stressed, "Insist on yourself; never imitate. ... Shakspeare will never be made by the study of Shakspeare."

The Sovereign Family

Individual sovereignty refers to the belief that each person has the right to govern themselves and make their own choices without interference from others. This principle can have a positive impact on family life and community in a number of ways.

First and foremost, individual sovereignty allows for the development of strong, independent individuals who are capable of making responsible decisions and taking care of themselves and their loved ones. This can lead to stronger, more functional families in which each member is able to contribute and support one another in a meaningful way.

Furthermore, when individuals are able to govern themselves and make their own choices, they are more likely to take ownership of their actions and the consequences that come with them. This can lead to a greater sense of responsibility and accountability, which can have a positive impact on the community as a whole.

Individual sovereignty also promotes the development of virtues such as self-discipline, self-reliance, and self-control. These virtues, when practiced by individuals, can lead to a more orderly, peaceful, and harmonious community.

Additionally, when individuals are able to freely express their true will and follow their own path, they are more likely to find fulfillment and satisfaction in their lives. This can lead to a more content and satisfied community, where individuals feel a sense of purpose and meaning.

Sovereign Psychology

Sovereign consciousness refers to a state of awareness in which an individual is fully self-aware, in control of their thoughts, emotions, and actions, and able to make conscious choices in alignment with their authentic state of being. It is a state of being in which the individual is free from the influence of the unconscious mind, societal norms and expectations, and is able to connect to their inner wisdom and intuition.

Carl Jung's psychological model of individuation is closely connected to the concept of sovereign consciousness. Jung believed that the ultimate goal of human development is to achieve a state of wholeness and integration in which the individual is able to reconcile the different aspects of their psyche. This process of individuation leads to an integration of the personality and a connection to the self, and it is through this connection to the self that the individual can achieve a state of sovereign consciousness.

In spiritual and mystical terms, sovereign consciousness can be described as a state of enlightenment or self-realization, in which the individual is able to transcend the ego-persona and connect to a higher state of consciousness. This state of enlightenment is characterized by a sense of inner peace, wisdom, and understanding, as well as a deep connection to the interconnectedness of all things.

Jung believed that the process of individuation is a lifelong journey and it is something that is unique to each person. It's a process of self-discovery and self-understanding that requires courage, honesty and commitment. It is a journey to the depths of the psyche, to the innermost aspects of the self.

> It's a journey that leads to the integration of the different parts of the psyche and ultimately to self-realization.

Declaration of the Sovereign Nation

We, the Sovereign Individuals, declare our independence from the oppressive forces that seek to control and manipulate us. We reject the notion that we are mere subjects to be ruled by commercial interest, and instead assert our inherent right to self-determination and self-sovereignty.

We recognize that true freedom is not just a legal concept, but a spiritual truth. We understand that true freedom comes from within, from being in control of our own thoughts, emotions, and actions. We reject the false belief that freedom can be granted or taken away by external forces, and instead recognize that freedom is our birthright as conscious, autonomous beings.

We assert our right to self-governance, to make our own decisions and chart our own course in life. We reject the notion that we are mere pawns to be controlled and manipulated by puppets of power, and instead recognize that we are the rightful masters of our own destiny.

We declare our independence from the constraints and impositions of institutions, and assert our right to be true to ourselves and our own unique path in life. We reject the belief that we *must* conform to unreasonable policies and mandates and instead recognize that true freedom comes from being true to one's own heart.

We recognize that true freedom and self-sovereignty are not just individual rights, but collective responsibilities. We commit ourselves to working together, to build a world in which all individuals are free to be true to themselves and to live in harmony with one another.

We, the Sovereign Individuals, declare our independence and assert our right to self-determination and self-sovereignty. We call upon all individuals to join us in this noble endeavor and to assert their own sovereignty. Together, we can create a better world, a world in which all individuals are free to live in harmony, respect, and prosperous cooperation with one another.

> "I know of no better life purpose than to perish in attempting the great and the impossible. The fact that something seems impossible shouldn't be a reason to not pursue it. That's exactly what makes it worth pursuing. Where would the courage and greatness be, if success were certain and there was no risk? True failure is shrinking away from life's challenges."

- Fredrick Nietzsche

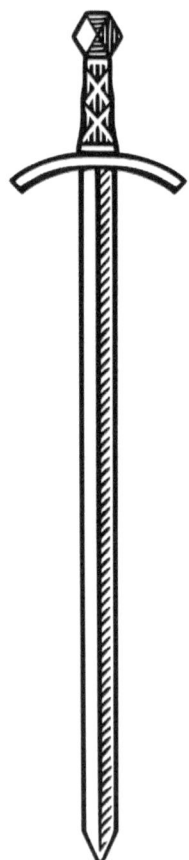

The New Nobility

In a world that often seems devoid of true virtue and integrity, the concept of nobility may seem like a relic of the past. Yet, the timeless ideal of nobility continues to captivate the human imagination, inspiring us to strive for something greater and more meaningful in our lives. But what does it truly mean to be noble in the 21st century?

From the courtly knights of medieval Europe to the landed gentry of the Renaissance, the definition of nobility has evolved and changed over time. Historically, nobility was often associated with wealth, birth, and status. But in today's society, these old definitions no longer hold the same weight.

This is why there is a need for a new definition of nobility, one that is relevant to the modern world and its new conditions. Our task now is to explore and redefine what it means to be noble in the 21st century. Through an examination of the qualities and character traits that make up a noble character, we will uncover what it truly means to be a person of integrity, courage, and honor.

The Old Definition of Nobility

The concept of nobility has a rich and varied history that spans centuries and continents. From the knights of medieval Europe to the feudal lords of ancient Japan, the ideal of nobility has taken many forms throughout the ages.

In the past, those who were born into noble families were considered to be part of an elite class. They were often wealthy landowners, with great power and influence over the lands and people under their control, equivalent to tech moguls today.

This old definition of nobility was based on the idea that those who were born into wealth and privilege were inherently superior to those who were not. However, this notion has been challenged and discredited in recent times, as the limitations of the old definition of nobility have become clear. Being a billionaire has nothing to do with being noble.

It is clear that a new definition of nobility is needed, one that reflects the values and aspirations of the Sovereign Nation.

The New Definition of Nobility

The old definition of nobility no longer holds the same relevance. But the ideal of nobility itself remains as important as ever, inspiring us to strive for something greater and more meaningful in our lives. So, what does nobility mean now?

The new definition of nobility is based on character traits and personal values. The key qualities of the new nobility include integrity, courage, dignity, and honor. These are the traits that define a person of character, and are the foundation for a life of purpose and meaning.

Integrity is the cornerstone of the new nobility, as it is the foundation for all other virtuous qualities. It is the inner strength that allows us to stand up for what we believe in, even when it is difficult or unpopular. Courage, dignity and honor are the building blocks that make up a noble character, allowing us to make a positive difference in the lives of those around us.

But how can we cultivate these qualities and live them out in our daily lives? The answer lies in our daily habits and routines. By focusing on our thoughts and actions, we can develop a noble character that is defined by integrity, courage, dignity, and honor. Through intentional effort and practice, we can become the new nobility and live a life of purpose and meaning.

The Noble Disposition

A noble disposition can be characterized by the following qualities:

Courage: A noble person is brave in the face of adversity and is willing to stand up for what they believe in, even if it means facing opposition.

Integrity: A noble person holds themselves to higher standards and consistently acts with honesty and integrity.

Understanding: A noble person is able to understand and relate to the experiences of others, showing depth of consciousness.

Honor: A noble person is confident and secure in their own abilities, but also acknowledges the strengths and contributions of others, avoiding arrogance or conceit.

Respect: A noble person shows respect for the human condition, and values dignity. Respect is the currency of a healthy society.

Graciousness: A noble person is courteous and kind in their dealings with others, radiating value and appreciation.

Responsibility: A noble person accepts responsibility for their actions and decisions, and takes a proactive approach to addressing their own mistakes.

Wisdom: A noble person possesses a deep understanding of the world and its complexities, and uses this wisdom to make informed and thoughtful decisions.

Generosity: A noble person knows when to be selfless and how to demonstrate generosity in both their thoughts and actions.

These qualities are not always easy to cultivate, but they are hallmarks of a noble disposition, and serve as a foundation for leading a virtuous and fulfilling life.

Cultivating the New Nobility

This is a journey of self-reflection and self-improvement, where we strive to become the best version of ourselves.

> Self-reflection is the starting point for cultivating the new nobility.

It is important to understand our own strengths and weaknesses, and to identify areas where we can grow and improve. This self-awareness will allow us to set meaningful goals and create a roadmap for our journey of self-improvement.

Once we have a clear understanding of where we stand, we can begin to develop the qualities of a noble character. Setting goals is a powerful tool for this process, as it helps us focus our efforts and track our progress. Seeking wisdom from those who embody the new nobility can also be a valuable resource, providing us with insights and guidance as we grow and develop.

Practicing generosity is another key component of cultivating the new nobility. Generosity is a powerful force for good, inspiring us to help others and make a positive difference in the world.

Finally, the role of community cannot be overlooked when cultivating the new nobility. By coming together with others who share our values and aspirations, we can create a culture of nobility that supports and encourages personal growth and development. In this supportive environment, we can inspire one another to live lives of purpose and meaning, becoming the new nobility together.

Benefits of the New Nobility

In our quest to cultivate the new nobility, we are not just striving to be better people, but to create a better world. By developing a noble character, we reap numerous benefits that extend far beyond our own lives.

> First and foremost, a noble character has a positive impact on our personal relationships.

People are naturally drawn to those who embody integrity, courage, dignity, and honor. These qualities inspire trust, respect, and deep connections with others, enriching our relationships and making our lives more fulfilling.

Leading by example is another important benefit of the new nobility. When we live out our values and embody the qualities of a noble character, we inspire others to do the same. We become role models and leaders, showing others what is possible and encouraging them to adopt a noble disposition of their own.

The impact of a noble society extends far beyond our personal lives, affecting the well-being and progress of the world as a whole. A society where people are guided by noble values is one that is more sustainable. It is a world where people are inspired to help one another, to create positive change, and to build a brighter future for all.

The new nobility represents a vital and necessary shift in our thinking about what it means to be a noble person in the modern world. By redefining nobility in terms of character and values, we open the door to a society where everyone has the opportunity to embody noble qualities and make a positive impact.

The future of our world depends on each of us taking responsibility for our own actions and striving to embody the qualities of the new nobility in our daily lives. It is up to us to lead by example, inspire others, and create a world that is built on human sovereignty and dignity.

The Sovereign Manifesto is the call to embrace the new nobility, and work together to create a brighter future for ourselves, our families, and our world. The time to act is now. Let us begin.

Twilight of a New Dawn

As the sun rises in the east, casting its golden light across the horizon, so too does a new dawn emerge for consciousness.

As the first rays of the sun pierce through the darkness, so too does a new light shine within the mind, illuminating the path ahead.

As the sun ascends higher into the sky, its warmth and radiance spreading far and wide, so too does consciousness expand, reaching new heights of understanding and insight. As the sun's light grows stronger, so too does our perception of this new reality become clearer, sharper, and more vivid.

Like the sun, the rising of a new consciousness is a powerful and transformative force, casting aside the shadows of ignorance and confusion, and bringing a newfound clarity and insight. As the sun's light illuminates the world around us, so too does the light of a new consciousness illuminate the truths of the world within us.

With every dawn, the sun rises anew, and so too does consciousness awaken, renewed and refreshed, ready to face the challenges and opportunities of a new day ahead.

This is the sound of the rooster's crow.

May the world awaken to a new dawn,
a new hope, a new flame.

Epilogue

The Sovereign Manifesto offers the reader a handful of valuable seeds to cultivate, seeds that bear a golden fruit. Cultivate these seeds and enjoy the fruits of Sovereignty.

In this book you have learned about the fundamental principles of power, politics and spirituality. You have caught the first glimpse of a new dawn. Now is the time to navigate yourself out of the staged social dynamics of a disordered world.

This manifesto offers a simple blueprint, one to make your own. Now it is your divine task to master the art of self-possession, defend against manipulation and influence, and ultimately, rise above the meaningless noise of the postmodern prison to achieve true sovereignty.

But the journey towards Sovereignty does not end here. *The Sovereign Manifesto* is not a guide to be read once and then forgotten. It is a tool and skill set to be studied, practiced, and refined over time. The principles and strategies outlined within these pages are not meant to be taken as gospel, but rather to be used as guidelines to help you on your journey.

Remember that Sovereignty is not a destination, but a constant process of self-discovery, self-improvement, and self-actualization. As you continue to grow and evolve, so too must your understanding of power and human nature.

We hope that this book has provided you with a valuable perspective and the tools to take control of your own life. May you continue to use your newfound knowledge to achieve your goals and maintain your Sovereignty in the ever-changing world.

The end of the book marks the beginning of your journey towards Sovereignty.

Oath of the Spiritual Sovereign

As a Sovereign, I am anointed the divine ruler of my land, appointed by the Gods themselves to lead and guide my Kingdom.

My right to rule is not earned through mortal means, but rather bestowed upon me by the Gods, as a symbol of their favor and protection. The Gods have spoken through the oracles, and their will is clear: I am anointed, a living vessel for the divine on earth.

My rule over my consciousness is absolute. Amongst my Kingdom, my authority is unchallenged. I am Sovereign, responsible for the well-being and prosperity of my Kingdom, for the protection of my land and for the maintenance of Ma'at (balance and harmony) in the world.

I am the link between the world of the living and the world of the dead, and my rule is a sacred trust, bestowed upon me by the Gods themselves.

My word is law.

Sign

The primary source material for the chapter titled
Sovereign Politick: A legitimate critique,
came from the book:

Sovereignty:
The Origin and Future of a Political and Legal Concept
by: Deter Grimm

Spiritual Sovereignty Series

www.ingramcontent.com/pod-product-compliance
Lightning Source LLC
Chambersburg PA
CBHW060359080526
44583CB00012B/381